D1369359

20
$ecrets
to Money and
Independence

Also by Joline Godfrey

No More Frogs to Kiss:
99 Ways to Give Economic Power to Girls

Our Wildest Dreams:
*Women Entrepreneurs Making Money, Having Fun,
Doing Good*

**St. Martin's Griffin
New York**

20

$ecrets

to Money *and*

Independence

The DollarDiva's
Guide to Life

**Joline Godfrey,
CEO Independent Means**

To Kari and Kate: indie women with DollarDiva visions

20 $ECRETS TO MONEY AND INDEPENDENCE. Copyright © 2000 by Joline Godfrey. All rights reserved. Printed in the United States of America. No part of this book may be used or reproduced in any manner whatsoever without written permission except in the case of brief quotations embodied in critical articles or reviews. For information, address St. Martin's Press, 175 Fifth Avenue, New York, N. Y. 10010.

www.stmartins.com

Book design by Maura Fadden Rosenthal/Mspaceny.

ISBN 0-312-26279-5

First Edition: September 2000

10 9 8 7 6 5 4 3 2 1

Contents

Contents

Acknowledgments

A book begins as an idea, which is a fragile thing. It becomes a force—something tangible and real—when the writer, aided by friends, muses, teachers, family, and chance encounters, makes some sense of the insights and support, the criticism and reflections that shape the final product.

My support team for this book includes the women who are my inspiration for independence: my grandmother the dairy entrepreneur; my mother, who sent me out into the world to explore; my dear muse, Jane, who taught me the value of the **bold** idea; Margaret Chase Smith, the senator from Maine who was my childhood model of independence; Susie Ells, who taught me what running with the big dogs really means; and Linda Hill, Joan Peters, and Sally Helgesen, independent thinkers who feed my head, as well as my soul.

The team also included men who pushed and supported me to explore an independence I occasionally resisted: Rebel, Jerry, and John, all wonderfully decent and wise men who now sleep with angels; and Jim, in one of those unintended consequences, stretched my vision.

Jenny Lytle, Shula Vakil, Victoria Groves, Dia Rao, Brooke Espinoza, and Syndi Seid added hard labor, great ideas, and their own models of independence—and for their help I am truly grateful. And the entire IMI team—DollarDivas all—help make my writing possible.

Betsy Amster may be the most patient and tenacious agent ever to inhabit the wild world of publishing. Getting to the proposal stage for this book was a feat I had given up on more than once. She never conveyed doubt, and that made all the difference.

The tens of thousands of Y-Gen women I have met around

the world—from San Francisco to Sydney, from Boston to Buenos Aires, from Juneau to Jacksonville, and Duluth to Denver—are the true contributors to this book. Their questions, challenges, and experiences helped me to focus on the issues critical to their lives. And their wisdom, humor, and spirit inspired me to overcome those inevitable lapses when words were more elusive than rain in the desert.

What kind of grrl are you?

I was a tomboy and one of the guys. I grew up on a street full of boys where there was no pitty-patting around. I loved to play football, and I think I could have made a great star quarterback except, of course, that girls didn't play football back then. I got good grades, but not straight A's. And I had a paper route when I was twelve, mainly because I'd tagged along with my friend Phil on his paper route for so long that his boss finally asked me why I didn't have a route of my own. So I got one, and pretty soon I had a savings account, which I took very seriously because I loved knowing that if there was something I really, really wanted, I could buy it myself. And I've never stopped loving that feeling.

But you know what I wish I'd had? A coach. Not just for sports, but sort of a life coach; someone who would have encouraged me to be myself, helped me to accept myself as I was, and who could have helped me to harness my gifts. I believe that everyone has special gifts, talents, or skills that you've been given and that are unique to you. But there's a funny thing about gifts: we don't always recognize them in ourselves. In fact, what looks weird to you might just be the very thing that sets you apart and makes you wonderful. It might even be your gift.

The *DollarDiva's Guide* encourages you to embrace your weirdness. I love that. We're all weird to some degree. It's part of who we are, and I think that embracing our weirdness is about recognizing, accepting, and loving our gifts. In my case, perhaps part of my gift was football, and who knows, maybe, just maybe, with the right coach, I could have been the first female quarterback in the NFL.

Another part of my weirdness is this: I feel very, very, very strongly about never wanting to be dependent on anyone. I want to be able to do what I want; I never want anyone to have any kind of veto power over what I can or want to do. I guess you could say I'm passionate about my independence. It's what I strive for myself, what I wish for my daughter and my sons, and it's what I wish for you. And that feeling has been a huge force in my life.

It's what has caused me to do what I do, which is to teach women and girls to become financially independent. It's what I do at work when I'm wearing my Charles Schwab & Co. hat, and it's what I do in my spare time, when I spend many hours teaching low-income women and girls. I'm very involved with them, and I wouldn't trade that experience for anything. I suppose I'm a sort of coach to those women and girls, which is great, because everybody needs a coach. That's exactly what you've got right here, in the DollarDiva. I wish I'd had her when I was in high school—and, believe it or not, I can still use her advice, because the questions she asks and the issues she raises in these pages don't just go away when you turn twenty, or thirty, or even forty. We're always growing up, we're always trying to improve, and the $ecrets offered here can help you do that, and they can save you some time. Over the years, I've learned many of them. But it hasn't always been easy, and it's taken a lot of experience.

With this book, you'll learn these things earlier, which is great because these $ecrets are definitely in the earlier-is-better category. The *DollarDiva's Guide* says that's it's okay to be who you are. You're already great. That's strong stuff, and the sooner you learn it and take it to heart, the sooner you'll be on the way to the best you can be.

That earlier-is-better quality is also true in the financial part of your life, as you'll see when you read about growing your money-self in Part three. Once again, the earlier you start investing, the better off you'll be, and the impact of starting early is huge. Being financially independent—meaning you don't have to depend on someone else for money—is a great source of confidence. It's also something that's extremely important to me personally.

And it's something you have to do for yourself. I speak from experience here. Even with a famous financial guru for a father, I had to learn about investing on my own. Don't get me wrong: I started working for his company during the summer when I was sixteen, and he was encouraging and more than happy to teach me. But I had to want to learn, I had to do it on my own, and I had to make my own decisions. And you know what? His not doing it for me and encouraging me to do it myself was one of his greatest gifts to me, one for which I'm very grateful.

I have a $ecret of my own for you: after you've read this book and truly become an independent woman you can give something back. Maybe all you can do right now is volunteer your time, and that's wonderful. But it's only a start. Work toward writing a check to a cause that's near and dear to your heart, and after that, work toward being a leader. Serve on a board, start something new—make a difference. Maybe you're the only one who can do it. And if you do, you will be rewarded. Helping others is empowering—as you strengthen other people, you become stronger yourself.

It's been my experience that everything in life builds on itself. This book will help you begin to build on yourself. It can help you to develop a life plan, and when you do that—when you have goals and when you know where you want to end up—your life becomes intentional, instead of a series of accidents or luck.

So take these $ecrets to heart; take them seriously. I am, and even though I'm coming up on forty, I consider myself lucky to have them. You're even luckier, because you're getting them while you're young. And with them you can take off, you can dream dreams and make them come true—and you can be the wonder called you, right from the start.

—Carrie Schwab Pomerantz
Vice President for Consumer Affairs and
Head of the Women's Initiative for Charles Schwab

IT'S A PARTY!

You are invited

to a celebration for independent femmes.

Knowledge of the Twenty $ecrets required.

RSVP to www.dollardiva.com

or call (800) 350-1816

for location, time and other details.

BE THERE .

Introduction: Who IS the DollarDiva? and What Are Her $ecrets?

DollarDiva is the ultimate Indie Grrl. She's money smart, and a little sassy. She has attitude and she isn't afraid to show it. She's a little worldly, a little wise, which is not to say that she doesn't occasionally make a mess of things. But she's a learner and never makes the same mess twice!

DollarDiva is an icon, the spirit of Independent Means Inc., a company I started that specializes in products and information that support the financial independence of Y-Gen women. Dollar-Diva has her own website (check out dollardiva.com to catch her ongoing adventures and get her advice). She's present (in our hearts at least) at all Independent Means gatherings (Camp $tart-Up™, Club Invest™, the DollarDiva MoneyFairs and lots of other IMI events), and she's always coming up with some new idea for making sure her friends are able to tap into the Twenty $ecrets.

DollarDiva is also Everygrrl. She exists inside everyone on a journey of independence and self-discovery. The readers of this book, indie women all, are DollarDivas—and the $ecrets you are about to discover are simply tools for making your individual journey easier and more exciting.

The DollarDiva's BIG Secrets

If you get all your information from *Cosmopolitan* and *People* magazine, mainstream movies, or any 30-minute network sitcom, you might assume that the main events that make us women are:

1. getting our first period;
2. landing our first job;
3. going to the prom;
4. graduating from school;
5. becoming engaged;
6. getting married;
7. having a baby;
8. getting your first promotion.

Of course that isn't so—and throwing a party for DollarDivas is an attempt to introduce more relevant *rites of passage.*

The invitation to discover the Twenty $ecrets is open to surfer chicks and soccer jocks, grrlgeeks and girly girls, poets and prom queens, wild things and intellectuals—all DollarDivas en route to claiming a womanself, becoming separate individuals, taking part in communities and relationships, pursuing careers, families, and dreams.

In my work, I meet Divas from all over the world, poor and privileged, diverse in race, culture, and values, who nevertheless share common questions:

⊙ What will I *be?*

⊙ How will I get there?

⊙ How will I support myself?

⊙ How can I have my twin desires for work I enjoy and a family I love?

⊙ What do I stand for?

⊙ Do I have worth or value? Am I important?

⊙ How can I make a difference?

⊙ What will be the cost or the consequences of my choices?

> **The Divas I meet seem to be searching for how to be their own person, while being a part of the world, not apart from it.**

What I find intriguing is that though the questions are similar, the answers are as individual as the questioners. And binding them all is a common quest: the pursuit of independence. Not independence of the lone-eagle variety—femme against the world, as it were—but independence that coexists with a family, a network of friends, and colleagues at work, and that allows you to be a dreamer of dreams. In other words, the femmes I meet seem to be searching for ***how to be their own person, while being a part of the world, not apart from it.*** This book is for everyone struggling with that conundrum.

DollarDiva's $ecrets have been around for a long time. They are, in a way, our inheritance from the experiences of women who have sought independence and self-esteem over the ages. Knowledge of these $ecrets will give you passage into the *Dollar-Divas' Gala.* (You'll have to visit dollardiva.com to get the details of this fete.)

The $ecrets have been distilled from the lives of truly independent women. Such women share qualities—the $ecrets I refer to—that have been tested over time. The $ecrets are a gift. The collective widsom of women who went before us, these $ecrets offer us direction and possibility. The $ecrets are not absolute answers to specific questions, and you can not use them as you might a Oujia board. (Will I marry an Indian raja or work for the embassy in Istanbul? for example!)

These $ecrets will help you make decisions when you are most confused. And the $ecrets offer ways of being that are lasting. When the world seems most surreal and absurd, these $ecrets have timeless value, like a tourmaline from Tiffany's or a magenta sky you can hold in your mind's eye for an eternity.

The DollarDiva's $ecrets are gems that have survived in myth and story, passed on through the real lives of brave women. You'll see that none of the $ecrets can be acquired without some effort. Developing independence is an exhilarating process—but it isn't for everyone, and it isn't as easy as say, making popcorn. **To begin, take the quiz below, check all the answers that apply to you, and read on.**

Life Desires

- [ ] I want to be good.
- [ ] I want to be independent.
- [ ] I want to be different.
- [ ] I want to be my own person.
- [ ] I want to save the world.
- [ ] I want to ask questions.
- [ ] I want to be bad.
- [ ] I want to be protected.
- [ ] I want to belong.
- [ ] I want a prince.
- [ ] I don't want the weight of the world's troubles on my shoulders.
- [ ] I want answers.

Twenty $ecrets are the keys to YOUR independence. Discover the $ecrets, make them work in your own life, and join the company of independent women—DollarDivas with attitude.

Did you check more than five desires? more than seven? It's perfectly natural to check all of them—to feel confused about what you want. Resolving these challenging questions in a way that works for you is an integral part of the process of becoming independent in the presence of your conflicting needs and desires.

BIG $ecrets: Hidden in Plain Sight

To make this book an experience rather than just a prop on your bedside table, use it to design your own brand of independence. Independence is not for the faint of heart, and only grande dames can mistress all the $ecrets. To acquire *most* of the $ecrets is the work of a lifetime.

But you can begin by exploring each of the mega-secrets, the big ideas that lead us to the Twenty $ecrets that give passage into the company of independent women. These women make a difference, touch the world, remain forever in our memory—not because of the scent of their perfume, but from the power of their being, the boldness of their spirits.

Nancy Drew once observed that if you want to hide something, it is best hidden in the open—in a place so obvious it will be overlooked by any but the most discriminating investigator (indie grrls for example). The five BIG $ecrets have been hidden in plain sight over the eons.

Each of the BIG $ecrets is so obvious, so simple, that at first glance you are tempted to say, "Duh, I already know that."

And of course you do. But there is knowing and there is KNOWING. Genuinely independent people know the difference between the two. To be superficially aware of something is not the same as really KNOWING something—and that is why the BIG $ecrets have eluded so many people and why the Twenty $ecrets are only accessible to those who are truly on a quest for independence.

The Twenty $ecrets are the subtler aspects of each of the BIG $ecrets. They offer a deeper insight into the daily acts and visions of the most independent women among us. Mastering the subtler aspects of independence will make the five BIG $ecrets all yours.

The BIG $ecrets are:

1. **Accept Yourself.**
2. **Uncover Yourself.**
3. **Grow Your Money-Self.**
4. **Get Out of Yourself.**
5. **Take Care of Yourself.**

How to Uncover the $ecrets

The $ecrets, when explored bravely and understood deeply, will show the path to your true independent self. They are ageless formulas, you cannot be too young (or too old) to master them.

The Twenty $ecrets are woven into the five BIG $ecrets. To begin your quest, select one $ecret from each of the BIG $ecrets. Over time you can go back and explore more $ecrets as you shape and experience your growing independence.

Discuss the $ecrets with friends—explore the meanings and implications the $ecrets hold for each of you. Put the $ecrets aside and re-visit them every six months or so—see how (or if) they become true, for you; readjust as the times and your circumstances warrant. Send an e-mail to **dd@dollardiva.com** and let me know what the $ecrets are doing for you.

Sometimes $ecrets are packaged like fake designer watches sold on the street: they look good, but underneath the shiny metal is a layer of tin. One magazine may try to sell you "10 Secrets to Happiness" (wear the right lipstick, date the right icon, go to the right school, et cetera, and the world is yours); your favorite celebrity may share the "3 Secrets of a Successful Life" (stay thin, think only positive thoughts, don't eat meat); or your mother may give you the "Six Secrets of a Good Girl." They may all be right. Possibly happiness does have something to do with great makeup, positive thoughts, or exemplary behavior.

But the authentic BIG $ecrets are more concerned with helping you figure out success and happiness *for yourself* than with getting you to follow someone else's rules. Only people who can think independently, make their own decisions, and are brave enough to say no when everyone else says yes (or the reverse), can really know for themselves what happiness and success mean.

The Twenty $ecrets shared in this book will help the indie grrl who puts them to work be unique and special in her own right. Robert Frost wrote, "Two roads diverged in a wood, and I took the one less traveled by and that has made all the difference."[1] Independent women blaze their own trails and dare to take the road less traveled even when it scares them to death!

The BIG $ecrets are simply the door to the Twenty $ecrets. Enter them only if you are curious, courageous, and committed. Practicing the Twenty $ecrets is not an undertaking for one without a "dog with bone" tenacity—but if you can see clearly what's "in plain sight" you will enrich yourself—and the world around you—immeasurably.

---

1. Frost, Robert. *Early Frost.* Meyers, Jeffrey, ed. NJ: Castle Books, 1999.

BIG $ecret One:
Accept Yourself

You can spend decades learning to grow comfortable in your own skin. But why should you? Why worry if:

⊙ you said the wrong (or the right) thing;

⊙ you look right (whatever that means);

⊙ you belong or fit in;

⊙ you're approved of?

Making friends with yourself, coming to terms with your very own unique, possibly eccentric, certainly one-of-a-kind self is the work of a lifetime. But the earlier you can fathom this secret, the less energy (and bewilderment) you will spend later on.

You know people who fully accept themselves. They have a sense of humor, an inner calm about who they are and what they do. Angst is not part of the baggage they carry in their backpack or on their shoulders. They are not fraught with noisy anxiety.

The $ecrets that follow are all dimensions of self-acceptance that help shape the independent person and, not surprisingly, help create an attitude that defines you as unforgettable, showering you in a scent more powerful than CK's Obsession.

$ecret 1

Embrace
Your Weirdness

" Whatever is weird today will be fashionable tomorrow. . . . "
—Matthew W. Brink

Embracing your weirdness may seem like a strange place to begin, but what is independence if not an attitude? Weirdness is, in part, simply the expression of your individual attitude. According to my dictionary, one definition of weird is "of strange or extraordinary character." The term often connotes the feeling of something not quite right—or even negative—but as you'll see time and again, the new, the rare, the one of a kind, often appears strange or even dangerous . . . at first.

Life without a degree of weirdness would be extremely tedious. Indeed, in the early days of Ben & Jerry's Ice Cream Company, as the founders were making decisions that would eventually make their company one of the most successful—and unique—in the world, Ben and Jerry would often determine an action after answering the question, "Is it weird enough?" If the answer was no, they were probably behaving like any other humdrum company and would need to start over again.

Wanting to be like everyone else and to be an individual—*at the same time*—is wildly human. Some days you want to dress like everyone else and other days you look like you could be the early Madonna's psychic twin. But developing weirdness that sets you apart as an original—an independent thinker—is about more than your fashion statement or the way you color your hair this month.

Sometimes weird just means ahead of your time—or crowd. African American Bessy Cole, the first woman to run an aviation school—she was a pilot ahead of her time—was considered a little weird. Sometimes weird means, "You don't agree with me so you must be weird." Holding an opinion, especially if it's original or unpopular is the tattoo of an independent thinker. Sometimes weird means you sound different (if, say, you're Mexican in an Anglo school or an American in Australia). Your culture may not be the one with the largest representation, but it is part of what makes you unique—and, yes, a little weird to others.

Weird can also mean a willingness to try something new and different. In 1966, Margot Fraser returned home from a trip to Germany with five pairs of funny-looking shoes she had found while visiting her original homeland. She had serious problems with her feet and those clunky-looking things made her feet feel better.

She gave away pairs to a few friends and they, too, found that, though the shoes looked pretty weird, they felt great. Margot may have seemed a little weird at the time, giving away such ugly-looking shoes—but she was weird enough to get one of the world's largest and most popular footwear companies off the ground. Today she is the founder and CEO of Birkenstock, a company that makes over $800 million in annual sales a year. Nurturing her weirdness definitely paid off for Margot.

> **One definition of weird is "of strange or extraordinary character."**

And no doubt Jamila Hubbard felt pretty weird as a six-foot-one high schooler. But Jamila decided to capitalize on her weirdness and entered the National Business Plan Competition with an idea to design and sell clothing for tall teens. As one of the winners, she traveled from her home in Oakland, California, to Boston, Massachusetts, where she met some astonishing role models, was interviewed by the press, and had a chance to spend time with four other high school winners—also a little weird—who were all very much into creating their own destinies.

Weird also means one of a kind. I own a book about shoes. It shows pictures of ancient shoes (the shoes worn by Cleopatra, for example), shoes with high heels, dancing shoes, sensible shoes, and boots. There are over 1,000 photographs of shoes in this book. But the last section is my favorite: "One of a Kind Shoes." Gorgeous, wild shoes, dripping with originality. Surely if one could afford to own these shoes and wear them to a dance, some would sneer and call the shoes weird. Yet, they are simply unique and unfamiliar—and to the wearer, beautiful, exotic, and rare.

Weird is the fingerprint of your soul. Just as each of us has our own, individual set of never-to-be-repeated squiggles on the tips of our fingers, the weirdness you nurture gives you an identity that is one of a kind. So, if we agree that weird is to be treasured, how do we nurture it?

This Is Your Best Stuff—Don't Let It Be Beaten out of You

Some days the most attractive, seductive course of action is blending into the woodwork. Looking like, sounding like, and feeling like everyone else can be a great comfort—easy, no sweat. And blending in part of the time is fine. A chameleon survives because it can take on the color of its background and avoid notice. You need to do that to observe, listen, and learn. You also need a lower profile to rest and catch your breath.

But you know how bored you eventually get when too much sameness piles up. And the last thing you want to be is boring. It's ironic that often your best stuff—that part of yourself that is unique, special, and maybe a little weird—is the part that makes the world uneasy. That uneasiness shows itself in insidious, subtle ways. Little comments like: "Oh sure." Or: "That is so weird." Or: "Are you crazy?"

It might even be as slight as a raised eyebrow, perhaps a giggle when you are feeling vulnerable. (You think, "Is she laughing at me?") Or it could come in the form of a great public embarrassment. Maybe a coworker reacts too quickly to one of your ideas and doesn't get what you are trying to say. Or a parent, in a moment of frustration says, "Oh don't be so dramatic." Or worse, tells you "not to be foolish."

Valuing the *fingerprint of your soul* and not allowing it to be vanquished without a fight takes fortitude. And it's not easy to distinguish the true gems of weirdness that make you you from those aberrant moments of experimentation when you're trying on ideas or costumes to see how they fit. Not all weirdness is permanent.

WEIRD RULES
- **DON'T LET YOUR WEIRD-NESS BE BEATEN OUT OF YOU.**
- **EXPERIENCE, DON'T RESIST IT.**
- **RESPECT WEIRDNESS IN OTHERS.**

I remember feeling vindicated, finally, for my own weirdness one day in my early thirties. I had just been invited to join a product development task force at Polaroid, where I was employed as a social worker. The man heading up the project invited me into the group by saying: "I don't know exactly what I want you to do, Joline. I just want you to do whatever it is you do."

Oh yeah, that made sense. But I got it. As a social worker in a company full of engineers, I saw the world differently from the rest of the people in the group. Jerry Sudby, the officer in charge, knew this. He knew that my slightly different view of the world—my own special weirdness, if you will—would cause me to ask questions and make suggestions that the other people on the team wouldn't think of. Jerry actually wanted to *use* my weirdness to make his task force think outside the box. Redeemed at last.

But I was in my thirties before this happened. I had to hold on to my weirdness for a long time before I recognized its value. Now I see that my feelings of being alien—feelings I lived with for most of my life, sometimes painfully—were actually my best stuff. What makes you different, unique, special is YOUR best stuff.

Push It, Experience It, Don't Resist It

Sometimes our first instinct in the face of our weirdness is an attempt to hide it. "If people really knew how weird I am," we think, "they would never associate with me." But of course that's just fear at work, a terrorist attack on the mind. If you do detect some part of yourself that seems a little out of the ordinary, explore it.

So, maybe you're attracted to playing the tuba in the college band. Not exactly your ordinary pursuit, but what if you become the world's leading expert on the history of the tuba? Or have the best collection of tuba print music in the country? Or win every tuba-playing competition the music world offers?

Or maybe you're a more creative mathematician than anyone you know. No doubt there will be a green aura coming from some of your "friends." But what if you push your ability in math? Some of the best jobs in Hollywood these days are not in front of the screen, but among the ranks of mathematicians working on special effects, marketing scenarios, and animation.

Your weirdness is, in a way, one of the stories you have to tell about yourself. The women I know who are special (and truly memorable) are not "just like everyone else." They have some special knowledge, or expertise, or strength that they have developed.

My Favorite Weird Women

Linda Greenlaw: Fisherman, writer.

Lynne St. James: Race car driver.

Shanta: Storyteller.

Anita Perez Ferguson: Activist.

Maya Lin: Designer/Architect.

Anna Devere Smith: Performance Artist.

Allow Weirdness in Others

Watch yourself. Do you sometimes gossip about the actions of friends that seem weird?

It makes no sense to accept everything as perfectly reasonable. Some things are truly crazy (drinking a quart of vodka at a party, for example). And some things are too awful to be tolerated (hate crimes and racism). But if you want room to develop your own soul's fingerprint, you have to respect the same right in others. The next time you are about to join in some "isn't she weird" attack conversation, think twice. One femme's weirdness is another's special gift. And won't you feel foolish when the weird one you made fun of walks to the podium someday to accept the Nobel Prize in physics?

Independent women are made exotic by their weirdness, by their willingness to be unique. "Style" is another word for weird. It's shorthand for the courage to stand out, be different, stride off the beaten path. Whether the style is that of Sarah McLachlan or Mother Teresa, the statements one makes about oneself—in small ways and large—are the ways we have of distinguishing ourselves as independent souls.

There is, of course, a difference between an affectation (something you put on that doesn't quite "fit") and a true, integral, original part of yourself that might be considered a little, well, weird. Staying in touch with the difference and making sure you aren't affecting some manner or habit intended for show rather than as a real part of yourself is not easy work. Consider these "one of a kinds" and think about what the fingerprints of their souls are:

⊙ Donna Dubinsky, entrepreneur responsible for giving us the Palm Pilot

⊙ Vanessa Mae, classical/rock violinist

⊙ Brandi Chastain, soccer champion

Now think about women in your own life who seem to stand apart from the crowd—how would you describe the fingerprints of their souls?

⊙ Is it the issues that matter to them?

⊙ Do they wrap a gift so beautifully you never want to open it?

⊙ Is it how they make others feel at home wherever they are?

⊙ Is it how they hold themselves when telling a story?

⊙ Or is it simply that they do the unexpected and are not afraid to lead?

Few great leaders are without some distinguishing weirdness. Name your weirdness, embrace it, and lead with it.

Gear, Resources, and Actions for Nurturing Weirdness

At the end of each chapter I have created a whimsical list of resources and experiences—geared for independence as it were. For an ever growing list, you can refer to **www.dollardiva.com** for more ideas, and to add your own suggestions.

Check Out These Books

Alcott, Louisa May. *Little Women*. Boston: Penguin USA 1989.

Cary, Lorene. *Black Ice*. New York: Knopf, 1992.

Drucker, Malka. *Frida Kahlo*. Albuquerque: University of New Mexico Press, 1995.

Kingsolver, Barbara. *The Bean Trees.* New York: HarperCollins, 1991.

Paterson, Jennifer and Clarissa Wright. *The Two Fat Ladies Ride Again.* New York: Clarkson Potter, 1998.

Santiago, Esmeralda. *When I Was Puerto Rican.* New York: Vintage Books, 1994.

Wong, Jade Snow. *Fifth Chinese Daughter.* Seattle: University of Washington Press, 1989

Try These Organizations

American Mensa

Known as the high IQ society. To be eligible for membership a person must score in the top 2 percent of the general population on a standardized intelligence test. (817) 332-2600 or **www.us. mensa.org.**

American Yo-Yo Association

A venue for players and collectors interested in the yo-yo as an art and sports form for both amateurs and professionals. (707) 542-YOYO or **yotopia@sonic.net.**

International Beam Web Games

Weird is welcome here. This is a robot competition. (505) 667-2902.

Magical Youths International

An organization for young adults interested in magic. Publishes *Top Hat.* (219) 255-4747.

Visit These Web Sites

The Unofficial Soup Kitchen (**www.usk.org**) describes itself as "a poetry jamboree, and traveling minstrel show, a small press, a guerrilla community advocacy outfit, and a sprawling web site with an emphasis on being an inclusive venue for artists of all disciplines and community, where diversity and tolerance thrive."

www.teenvoices.com An interactive forum dedicated to challenging and changing the image of women in the media and advocating for teen women.

www.dollardiva.com Go to the "Independence Hall" columns and look up "Hollywood and Math" for an introduction to the positions that mathematicians have in Hollywood.

See These Videos

Antonia's Line, 1995, by Dutch filmmaker Marlene Gorris. The eccentric characters in this film all have their own unique view of life!

Benny and Joon, 1993, starring Johnny Depp.

Don Juan DeMarcos, 1995, directed by Jeremy Leven.

Housekeeping, 1987, directed by Bill Forsyth.

Try This

Interview five people you think of as weird but comfortable with themselves.

Think about what they say that runs like a theme through their conversations.

Inventory the qualities that might qualify you for weirdness.

Study them, explore them.

Make your own list. Who would you name to your Top Ten Weird and Wonderful Ones?

$ecret 2

Take Yourself Seriously

"To be demanding, one must also be demanding of oneself. Once people realize that you can hold your own, they will be happier to comply."
—Nathalie Baez

What's the difference between a rock star wannabe and holding an audience rapt at a live concert? What's the difference between a closet writer and a published author? What's the difference between imagining a business and putting yourself through college on the profits you made from the company you started? What's the difference between "maybe someday" and "yesterday I did?" **Independent women know. The difference lies in taking yourself seriously.**

Banish the following thoughts:

- ⊙ "I'm too young (or, I'm too old)."
- ⊙ "I don't know enough."
- ⊙ "I don't have enough experience."
- ⊙ "I'm not strong enough."

⊙ "I'm not smart enough."

⊙ "I don't know how."

These phrases are more terrorist attacks on the mind—and they do more to undermine femme achievements than any law or tradition. *Not taking yourself seriously gives others permission to do the same.*

A few years ago the Avon Foundation sponsored a study asking female business owners what they thought were their greatest obstacles. Most people expected that "access to capital (money)" would be cited most often. But the number-one obstacle that these women said they faced was "being taken seriously." This is a real issue for femmes in pursuit of economic and social independence. But those who are taken seriously take themselves—and their sisters—seriously.

How Seriously Do YOU Take YOURSELF?

1. __T__F I always speak up and rarely have to be told to "speak louder please."

2. __T__F I write down my ideas and act on them as plans, not merely dreams.

3. __T__F I ignore people who laugh at my ideas.

4. __T__F I participate in debates and conversations, confident that my views matter.

5. __T__F I challenge people who dismiss my ideas as silly, naive, or unimportant.

6. __T__F I don't date people who don't take me seriously.

7. __T__F I write letters to the editor.

8. __T__F I project dignity by the way I walk, sit, and dress.

9. __T__F I almost always trust my intuition.

10. __T__F I do my homework, researching carefully anything I'm really interested in.

Five or more trues checked means you're reasonably willing to listen to yourself and can select another $ecret for deeper study. Five or less means you probably need a remedial class before we let you into any advanced celebrations of independent women.

I run seminars for the financial novice. Usually I start by running through a checklist of tasks to master by the age of 20. They're basic things: balancing a checkbook, opening a savings account, managing a budget, setting aside money for philanthropy, as well as other long-term goals. But there's always at least one femme who zones out, and when I ask her if she has completed any of the tasks on the list, she will say (always in a tiny little voice), "Not yet, I'm really too young."

I have two young friends, Sharique and Zaheen, whom you'll get to know in a later chapter. These two young men were trading-card tycoons at the ages of 10 and 12. They've got my list covered and then some—how come they don't think they're too young? They take themselves seriously.

And oh, about that tiny voice: How often are you asked to speak up? Do you think when Madeline Albright was sitting in meetings at the United Nations anyone had to tell her to "Speak up?" Or do you recall any interviewer who's had to ask Rosie O'Donnell to, "Speak a little louder please"?

Taking ourselves seriously shows in hundreds of subtle ways: the way we project our voice, the initiative we show in learning and mastering new things, our willingness to take some risks, and our **visibility.**

Trusting yourself is the first step in taking yourself seriously.

> ◎ If you feel you have nothing to say, your voice will be a whimper in the wind.
>
> ◎ If you think you are not important, you will be invisible.
>
> ◎ If you have no confidence in your own opinions, you will not listen to your inner voice.

Terrorist Attacks on the Mind

"I'm too young (or, I'm too old)."
"I don't know enough."
"I don't have enough experience."
"I'm not strong enough."
"I'm not smart enough."
"I don't know how."

So what can you do if you show any of the symptoms of not taking yourself seriously?

Torture Yourself

Let's face it, trusting that *maybe* you have something to say, *maybe* you have an opinion worth listening to, and getting it out in the air, can be a kind of torture. But until you begin to test yourself—however painfully—you will live with the suspicion that you ARE NOT worth listening to or worth taking seriously.

Those first few leaps into the unknown, when you test your own worth, can be feverishly dreadful—but did you ever see any road built without a little sweat? So get over it. Practice taking yourself seriously, and you'll convince others they should take you seriously, too.

The history of thoughtful, serious women is littered with tales of their ridicule, censure, dismissal. Think of how Madonna or Janet Jackson have been vilified for things they have said or done. Hilary Rodham Clinton has been dissed and dumped on. But all these women continue living their lives certain that what they feel inside matters. And they do not seek approval from others for their ideas. They take themselves seriously. Indeed, these women thrive on the energy that comes from defending their most serious values and aims—however inexplicable those concerns may be to others.

Independent femmes are often undermined by being labeled "emotional" or "drama prone" or "melodramatic." It's a sneaky way for others to dismiss the passion of one's commitments. But truly independent spirits stand up for and defend their ideas until *finally* others are forced to take their ideas and actions seriously, too.

Get a Buddy and Make a Pact

Sometimes it's easier to see how others undermine the best part of themselves than it is to recognize this tendency in our own behavior. Find a friend (only a good friend will really work for this) who agrees to call you on your behavior when you act like someone who should NOT be taken seriously. Your friend should agree to let you do the same for her. Then stick to your pact. This is no time to be nice. Your very essence is at stake here. If you don't take yourself seriously how can you ever be independent?

Master Something, Anything

Knowing a lot about something gives you confidence. When you know a subject stone cold, you begin to develop the confidence to hold opinions, take stands, and take yourself seriously. You can't know everything about everything, but find a subject you can master. (Or do I mean mistress? Whatever.) Maybe you already know more than anyone in America about the value of Hello Kitty products or perhaps you play golf better than any of your friends. Whatever expertise you nurture will help you take yourself seriously in at least one area and may help you to trust yourself in other realms where you may not be an expert, but just a reasonably intelligent person, worthy of holding an opinion.

And about that word "enough." Who calls the shots on what is enough? As in smart enough, old enough, experienced enough, strong enough . . . The word is a virtual saboteur. Unless you call the shots on what is ENOUGH, you will always be waiting for someone else to set the standard for you. Take yourself seriously and decide for yourself when enough is enough!

Study Serious Women

There are a few ways to accomplish this. Check out C-SPAN. This cable channel covers live actions in the House and Senate, committee meetings, speeches of note relevant to the workings of the United States. It is, in a way, our window to the most serious work of politics. C-SPAN runs pretty much round the clock, so you can get quite a strange sampling of behavior! But observe in particular the women who make speeches or debate issues.

It is a joy to watch such people as Congresswoman Eleanor Holmes Norton or the former president of the National Women's Political Caucus, Anita Perez Ferguson. Often C-SPAN covers the speeches of Madeline Albright or those of female dignitaries from other countries. Notice how they use their smiles sparingly—when they *intentionally* want to share humor or warmth as part of their message, not as the whole message.

Examine women you admire. Do they giggle inappropriately? Probably not.

Lose the Smile

Of course I don't mean you should never smile. But be discriminating. Take an anthropological survey: review magazines, watch a few television shows, observe your friends and other women in restaurants and shopping malls. When do they smile? When they want approval, of course! Ever notice how coy those smiles can be? How much giggling accompanies the simplest interaction when you're nervous, trying to attract that sweet amour, or you just want to make sure you are *liked*?

Now try the same exercise with men. Check out the clothing ads in your favorite magazine. Are they smiling coyly? Not so often. Watch the news. When men deliver information, are they looking for approval with a cute little smile or a giggle? Not likely.

Obviously I don't long for a new generation of sourpusses—what the world needs is a little more cheer, not a lot of Grim Gertas. But when you compare the smiling activity of men and women, it's easy to see that men often hold and present themselves in ways that say: "I'm a presence. I take myself seriously and you should, too." (Now granted, they often overrate their importance, but that's a different conversation altogether.)

Think about what YOU take seriously: I don't think for a moment that we should be copying the male of the species. (Lord knows they have flaws of their own.) But I am aware that sometimes women undermine their most powerful presentations of self by smiling too much, giggling inappropriately, and giving the message—however unintentionally—that, "What I am saying is sort of humorous, not seriously thought out, not deeply intended."

The smile, that glorious mode of communication, the simple movement of muscles that has brought us attention, provocative advances, tires changed for our "helpless little selves," and all manner of rewards from daddies and doormen alike, is a gesture the independent femme uses judiciously.

The next time you're at a restaurant, spend some serious time people watching. See those women smiling adoringly, hanging on every word the guy across from them is uttering? When will guys catch on that behind those sappy smiles are fervent wishes that they would just stop talking and ask a few questions?! They *won't* catch on until we stop reinforcing their behavior. Women men take seriously are those who engage with them, who have serious conversations and DON'T try to win approval at every turn. Independent women have a life, a point of view, and thoughts, and they aren't afraid to share their opinions, even when approval is NOT likely to be forthcoming.

In $ecret Eighteen you will learn about building "gatekeeper"

> **HOW TO TAKE YOURSELF SERIOUSLY**
> - **TORTURE YOURSELF WITH PRACTICE.**
> - **GET A BUDDY, MAKE A PACT.**
> - **MASTER SOMETHING.**
> - **STUDY SERIOUS WOMEN.**
> - **RETHINK "ENOUGH."**
> - **LOSE THE SMILE.**

friendships. That will be easier to do if you get a grip on excessive smiling. Independent femmes find it embarrassing to be seen with gigglers and chronic smilers. Maybe we think that not being taken seriously is contagious—and in a way it is. If I am seen with someone who wears a constant foolish grin on her face—regardless of the content of the conversation around her—I could be regarded as a little empty-headed, too.

Now that may be crazy, but there it is. So, back to that buddy. Make sure one of the things you do for each other is to observe whether or not your smiling muscles are in overdrive or if you present yourself in such a way that your expression mirrors the content at hand!

Gear, Resources, and Actions for Taking Yourself Seriously

Check Out These Books
Estes, Clarissa Pinkola. *Women Who Run With the Wolves: Myths and Stories of the Wild Woman Archetype.* New York: Ballantine Books, 1995.

Kingston, Maxine Hong. *Woman Warrior: Memoirs of a Girlhood Among Ghosts.* New York: Vintage Books, 1977.

Woolf, Virginia. *A Room of One's Own.* New York: Harcourt Brace, 1991.

Visit These Web Sites
www.womenconnect.com

www.women.com

www.her-online.com

www.feminist.com

www.smartgirl.com

See These Videos
Elizabeth, 1998, starring Cate Blanchett.
My Brilliant Career, 1979, starring Judy Davis.
The Piano, 1993, starring Holly Hunter.

Try This
Name 10 women in literature who take themselves seriously; list 10 who don't. Which characters do you most resemble?

"Always asking permission comes from a 'less worthy than' perspective. If you feel you are worth it (emotionally and financially) it is worth going ahead with actions... even those that break new ground or rules."
—Phyllis Lerner

Ask Forgiveness, Not Permission

I used to ask permission for everything. I used to follow the rules—all the time. I used to end all sentences with, "okay?" I was not, I think, a rebellious kid. In fact, I remember hearing adults talk about what a nice child I was. I was quiet. I read a lot. Adults seem to think silence and obedience are good qualities in children.

Breaking the Rules

I can't tell you exactly when I began to change. I suppose the older I grew, the less the world made sense, and the harder it was to keep quiet and follow rules blindly.

Then a funny thing started to happen. I began to notice that the people I admired most were often rule-breakers, too. Nice people, not terrorists of any kind, but people who questioned authority, who asked, "Why?" or "What if?" instead of ending every sentence with "okay?" Among my heroes and heroines:

- **Susan B. Anthony.** She spent her entire life asking why women couldn't vote. She broke the law by voting in her hometown of Rochester, New York, in 1872. And it wasn't until 1919, thirteen years after her death, that women in the United States finally were given the right to vote. Her rallying cry, when it came to her cause, was "Failure is impossible."

- **Martin Luther King, Jr.** In the face of anger, humiliation, and violence, he persevered. He looked at the "rules" dictating the behavior of people of color and said in effect, "I don't think so."

- **Amelia Earhart.** Amelia broke new ground by learning to fly and by flying wild, dangerous missions. In the end, her passion cost Amelia her life, but her fire still burns and she's remembered as someone who defied convention to pursue her dreams—and opened doors for other women.

- **Edwin Land.** The inventor of the Polaroid Land Camera and instant photography, Land dropped out of college to pursue his dream. He challenged the laws of physics to make something new happen in photography that, up until he invented instant photography, was considered impossible. Land's advice to others was to "spend your life trying to solve impossible problems." Those were the efforts worth spending sweat, blood, and tears on. The less courageous among us, he maintained, would worry about the less challenging problems.

Did any of these people ask permission to pursue their dreams? They did not. But they did share some positive qualities.

Bold Goals

My heroes and heroines didn't waste time on trivial things. They understood that there isn't enough time to sweat the small stuff!

A Clear Sense of What's Important to Them

None of my folks were wimps. If they believed in something, they stood up for it—regardless of what others thought. Each of them was ridiculed, harassed, and worse.

Willingness to Take the Heat

It takes courage to speak out, express unpopular views, and challenge what "everyone" knows to be true. But my heroes and heroines all were willing to resist popular opinion and weather opposition until they had reached their goals.

A Higher Purpose

Pursuing their dreams for their own gain or glory wasn't enough for any of my heroes and heroines. They wanted greater impact on the world than mere personal fame or wealth. It made sense to endure hardship, ridicule, and hard times, if they felt some greater good would result.

Not everyone possesses these qualities; they come from strong character, courage, and practice. But they were qualities I wanted to develop, even if I didn't know how to do so, or what my own higher purpose was for many years.

Later, after graduate school, I went to work for a company that valued initiative and gave people opportunities to try a variety of jobs, regardless of formal training. The company fundamentally believed that, if trusted and supported, people would always surpass expectations.

I flourished in this atmosphere. In homes and companies that nurture trust, rules tend to be less important—you are expected to act responsibly, so usually you do. But this is also the kind of environment that encourages risk taking. And I took risks.

As time passed, I became bolder and bolder. In the middle of a new project I wanted the input of one of the top design heroes in the world. But I did not have the authority to hire him and to go ahead and do so would have been seen as impulsive at best and rude at worst.

I went to the person I reported to at the time and told him what I wanted to do. He shook his head, smiled, and quietly said to me, *"Better to ask my forgiveness, not my permission."* He fully understood that what I wanted to do breached good protocol in the company. At the same time, he felt my idea was a sound one. There are some things that you have to do—and for which you must take full responsibility—with the hope that the outcome will be sufficiently positive to warrant forgiveness for not having asked beforehand.

I went ahead and hired the design genius to come in as a guest consultant. I didn't make myself real popular in some quarters, but I achieved my goal and moved the project (and the company) forward a little. This time my willingness to ask forgiveness, not permission paid off. But that doesn't always happen.

Rebellion versus Making a Stand

How can you tell if you are being rebellious and breaking rules merely to get your own way, or if you are making a stand for something important? And when does it matter? Women who know $ecret Three keep the map below in their mind's eye.

Think of a situation (say a school board policy or a practice enforced by the owner of a local bank) and place yourself in the map according to the following questions:

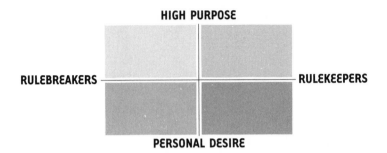

⦿ Is what you want to change concerned with some personal need or wish or is it something that will make a difference to the whole community, your friends, or your family? Based on the answer to this question, place yourself in either the "northern hemisphere" of the map or south of the "equator."

⦿ Do you want to achieve the goal by keeping to the existing "rules" or are you ready to break rules to achieve your goal? Now you can determine if you belong to the left or right of the center longitude. (If the target of change encourages open discussion of all subjects, you'd be *following* the rules by opening conversation. If not, you'll be on the verge of rule-breaking.)

If you located yourself in the lower left-hand side of the map, you may have a bit of a selfish streak, going after your own needs at any cost, caring little about the needs of others. (Or it may just mean that you so desperately need to change the policy that offends you that breaking a rule at any cost *is* actually in your best interest!)

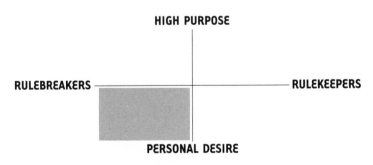

A placement in the upper right-hand corner of the map may indicate that you respect tradition and authority and are willing to hang on to them at the expense of significant change. Sometimes that's a great stabilizing influence, but other times it's an impediment to change that may be needed. (Someone who never breaks the rules and has a high moral rationalization for their action or nonaction may be a real obstacle to change that improves the welfare of all.)

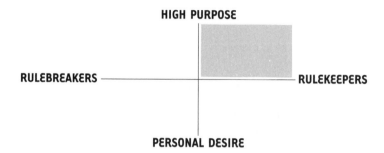

Placement on the upper left-hand corner of the map may mean you're a change agent, someone who questions authority and is ready to upset the applecart for the "greater good" of the group. A change agent can be valuable in a situation that needs change, but if impulsive, can also be a real troublemaker! (If you have always respected authority and are now willing to "break the rules," expect a change in how the people you threaten will react to you.)

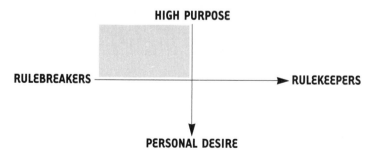

Did you find yourself in the lower right-hand corner of the map? That may indicate a fearfulness of anything that jeopardizes your personal status quo. Fear and rigidity are characterized in this area. (If fear has always prevented you from learning or discover-

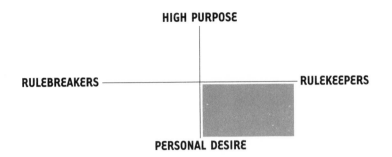

ing new information that could improve your life, this may be a problem. . . .)

Smart, independent women tend to lead lives in which some situations require supporting tradition and building community, others require their most rule-breaking courage, and still other situations demand a little personal selfishness. Suppose you're being treated badly by a jerk boyfriend but you think making a big deal of his behavior would scare him away. You might want to consider placing yourself firmly in the lower left-hand quadrant and making personal concern your number-one issue for a time.

In truth, independent women, over the course of their lives, spend time in each of the quarters of the map. Watching your patterns will give you an idea of how comfortable you can be with this $ecret!

The Map and Creativity

I don't mean to encourage wholesale rebellion or reckless behavior. But unless we sometimes break rules, we make no leaps of imagination, and we can't make the creative breakthroughs that have driven human beings since the Stone Age.

Early sailors defied conventional wisdom and risked fortunes to test the notion that the earth was round and not flat. Creative people seem constitutionally unable to "leave well enough alone." Every new movement in art, literature, politics, social change, and invention has come about because someone asked "What if?" and "Why not?"

To create means to break out, to break through. Madonna created a sensation in her early days because she didn't act like any woman we had ever seen before (except perhaps Cleopatra). She intentionally broke rules and that made people crazy. She reached for new ways to express herself and for better or worse introduced new ideas about performance that the entertainment world now seems to take for granted.

Breaking Rules is at the Heart of Creativity

Daring to break with tradition, to try new methods that are strange, unconventional, and risky—and knowing when to do so—is what helps bring invention into the world.

I tend to find myself in the upper left-hand corner of that map more often than not. I've grown up hearing people refer to my "weird ideas." But for that reason, I like working with a team of people whose makeup includes some folks who live more consistently in the upper right-hand corner, while maybe one member of the team is a real wild card and falls in the lower left-hand quadrant, with the other wild card falling in the lower right-hand section. When all these *players* are part of a team, the potential for creative tension and differing points of view is high—and can lead to a very creative outcome!

Breaking Rules for Breakthrough Developments

Fanny Farmer and Betty Crocker might not recognize Jordana Olszewski's unconventional cookies but they sell all the same! At 17, Jordana noticed the seeming contradiction between the growing demand for nutritional supplements and the constant craving of the American sweet tooth. Putting together the two things didn't seem strange to her and the result was a business called Cookie Craze: custom-made cookies that offer vitamin and mineral enriched supplements in irresistible cookies.

Jordana didn't break any "laws" to create her healthy cookies, but she didn't slavishly follow the rules of any cookbook either. And, in a way, she was the forerunner of all the other "health bar" cookies on the market today. Daring to "go outside the box" feeds the forces of creativity.

If I am going to consistently break rules and ask forgiveness, I want to know someone on my team will balance my tendencies by asking tough questions and holding out for a more conventional solution. Often the tension between their way and mine forces something wonderful to emerge.

Rule-breaker Role Models

I have taken pains to emphasize that I don't encourage breaking rules for the sake of a lark (okay, well maybe sometimes, if it's harmless enough). When I go back to "ask forgiveness," as sometimes I must, I want a story to tell, a reason I chose to take the risks I did.

I may not *be* forgiven, and others may not agree with me, but if I break rules to get something done, I'd better have a good reason for doing so. Rules are critical to making a decent society work. (I like having cars stop at pedestrian walks, for example. That's a rule that makes me feel I am in a safe and sane community.)

So lest you still think I'm encouraging you to follow in the footsteps of such notorious rule-breaking women as Bonnie Parker (of Bonnie and Clyde infamy) and Lizzie Borden (famed for whacking her stifling parents with an axe), here's a list of women who had the courage to think outside the box, fight against conventional wisdom, and break rules, but who managed to do so by taking the *high ground* most of the time.

- ☉ **Sojourner Truth.** In *1843,* she repeatedly challenged laws to advocate for the emancipation of slaves and women. Born into slavery and set free in 1827, Sojourner spent her life breaking rules to free others.

- ☉ **The Lowell Mill Girls.** Throughout the 1830s they went on strike when the mills they worked for announced wage cuts of up to 15 percent. Up to that point, the young women had been well behaved—and exploited.

⊙ **Elizabeth Blackwell.** Though considered immoral and laughable, Blackwell insisted on entering Geneva College as the first female medical student. The school made the experience horrific for her—but she defied them all and completed her studies in 1849 to become the first modern woman to graduate from medical school.

⊙ **Margaret Sanger.** In 1916, Margaret and her sister broke the Comstock Law and opened the first birth control clinic in Brooklyn, New York. Before it was closed— just 10 days later—the sisters had seen over 500 women, demonstrating the powerful need for their service and strengthening their conviction that this work needed to be done. Finally, thanks to her undaunted willingness to break rules, by 1938, the Comstock Law was dismantled and the sisters opened a network of more than 300 birth control clinics around the country.

⊙ **Althea Gibson.** In 1950, Althea became the first African American to play in the U.S. Open National Championships at Forest Hills. Althea's act of breaking "the color line," is in no small part the reason we watch the performances of athletes Venus and Serena Williams today, little remembering what has made their presence so "normal."

⊙ **Rosa Parks.** In 1955, when told by a bus driver in Montgomery, Alabama, to give up her seat to a white man, Rosa refused. This small act of rebellion sparked a massive boycott by African Americans against the bus company. Six years later, the Supreme Court sided with Rosa and those fellow Americans who felt the rule was wrong, and forced a change in the law.

- ⊙ **Iris Rivera.** In 1977, Iris was fired because she refused to make coffee for her boss. Her decision spurred other office workers to stop making coffee as well. When Women Employed organized a group of women to march to Iris's old office and present her boss with a bag of used coffee grounds, they reclaimed her old job and helped bring about a sweeping change in attitudes about women's roles in the workplace.

- ⊙ **Wilma Mankiller.** In 1985, Wilma defied tradition and became the first female Principle Chief of the Cherokee Nation. Though resented by many for her bold leadership, she pushed through new training, education, and health service programs. And she established and managed a multimillion dollar community development effort that fundamentally changed the lives of Cherokee Nation citizens.

Unforgiven

It would be naive to leave this chapter without addressing the consequences if, having broken the rules for something you believe in and having later asked forgiveness, the world (or specific people in the world) still thinks you are wrong or that you've done something wrong.

You are ostracized, outcast, unpopular. Behavior has consequences and the words "I'm sorry" fall flat if used too often or if not sincere. Sometimes we break rules and truly aren't sorry—certain that we've done the right thing. Then what? How does one live with the fallout from action taken that is not embraced by family, friends, coworkers, the public? Sometimes you must endure. You live with the consequences of your actions.

Maya Lin was a senior at Yale University when she submitted her design for the Vietnam Veteran's Memorial. Her concept was so unique, so rule-breaking in the tradition of war memorials, that the wrath of Congress, the Veterans Administration, and thousands of Americans was focused on her for several years. Most people have come to love and honor her vision, but she had to endure censure, scathing newspaper articles, the potential loss of reputation, and the possibility that she would become too "hot" for anyone else to hire her and commission her designs. At 21, her career could have been over because she saw the world through different eyes. Her vision looked forward and not back, she worked outside the box, not in it.

Today, almost 20 years later, Maya Lin is one of the most successful and celebrated designers of the new century. But it was not an easy path. Had she caved in to her critics, followed the rules on all subsequent design opportunities, her gift would have been lost.

Sometimes to break rules—to act and to see the world with original eyes—is a painful and serious choice. But some people would rather die than "follow the pack." They can't breathe if they're not allowed to think independently. Breaking rules carries responsibility and consequence. Independent women know this and choose their battles wisely!

Gear, Resources, and Actions for Asking Forgiveness, Not Permission

Check Out These Books

Battle, Kemp. *Hearts of Fire: Great Women of American Lore and Legend.* New York: Three Rivers Press, 1997.

Chang, Pang-Mei Natasha. *Bound Feet & Western Dress, A Memoir.* New York: Doubleday, 1996.

Evans, Ed D., Susan B., and Joan P. Avis, Ph.D. *Women Who Broke All the Rules: How the Choices of a Generation Changed Our Lives.* Naperville: Sourcebooks Trade, 1999.

Hirschman, Albert O. *Exit Voice and Loyalty: Responses to Decline in Firms, Organizations, and States.* Boston: Harvard University Press, 1970.

Jacobs, Thomas A., and Jay E. Johnson. *What are My Rights?: 95 Questions and Answers about Teens and the Law.* Minneapolis, MN: Free Spirit Publishing, 1997.

Mills, Kay. *From Pocahontas to Power Suits: Everything You Need to Know about Women's History in America.* New York: NAL/Dutton, 1995. One quote from this book: "Well behaved women rarely make history!"

Turner, Nancy E. *These Is My Words: The Diary of Sarah Agnes Prine, 1881–1901: A Novel.* New York: Regan Books, 1998.

White, Kate. *Why Good Girls Don't Get Ahead . . . but Gutsy Girls Do: 9 Secrets Every Working Woman Must Know.* New York: Warner Books, 1995.

See These Videos

Maya Lin: A Strong Clear Vision, 1995, directed by Frieda Mock. Call (310) 459-2116 for more information.

Norma Rae, 1979, starring Sally Fields.

Silkwood, 1983, starring Cher.

Try This

Keep a journal of how and when you make decisions about issues that matter. Do you get approval before you make a move? How do you think about your actions and what you can and cannot do to "change rules"?

4 $ecret

Get Loud

" Paddle, kick, scream, jump, swim, fight. Do whatever it takes to let your voice be heard and to let your presence be felt in a room. Stay quiet and remain anonymous."
—Jessiny Nueces

"What? What did you say? Would you say that again please? Could you speak up? I'm sorry, I can't hear you. . . . *I can't hear you*. . . . I CAN'T HEAR YOUUUUU. . . ."

Is this what happens when you speak? Nothing so gives away the soul of a frightened being than that little pea voice stuck inside that no one can hear. What's the worst that can happen if you are heard? Right, someone will think you are:

    a. wrong,

    b. stupid, or

    c. present.

If you pretend to be invisible with a tiny little voice, maybe no one will notice you, pick on you, catch you at whatever gaffe you imagine you will commit. Now get this: independence is expressed in the voice. When you project: "**I AM AN INDEPENDENT PERSON**," others tend to agree with you. "I . . . am . . . an . . . independent . . . person," on the other hand, *is not convincing.*

Your feelings about yourself are often revealed in the pitch, the volume, the strength, and the firmness of your voice. Are you hesitant, tentative, unsure if the things your inner voice says can be accepted by the cold outer world? Self-doubt reveals itself in the voice others hear.

ESSENTIALS OF VOICE
- **HOW IT HITS THE WORLD.**
- **WHAT IT DOES.**
- **WHEN IT'S USED.**

Developing Your Voice

But you are, after all, in charge of your voice. There are things you can do. Until you fully master/mistress the BIG $ecret of Self-Acceptance (trusting your inner voice), you can discipline your outer voice to project self-acceptance. And like a cassette in an endless loop, it will come back to you, helping you acquire real self-acceptance of your inner self. The three elements of developing your voice are:

1. the way in which your voice hits the world (sound, volume, pitch, clarity),
2. what it does (the reason you exercise it), and
3. when it's used. (Sometimes a silent voice is the most eloquent of all.)

How It Hits the World

Most of us hate to hear ourselves on tape. (For some reason the sound is completely distorted by how good or bad we feel about ourselves.) So to figure out how you really do sound you can:

a. *Ask your friends.* Make sure they know that this is no time to be polite. Truth (when requested) is often the sincerest support a friend can give.

b. *Watch how others respond to your voice in different situations.* This can be tricky if you expect bad responses when you open your mouth—try to be very clear about what you are seeing.

c. *Get an assessment from a speech coach.* Almost every school has one—if not, check with a drama coach, the choral leader at church, anyone who is involved with voice.

Ask these people to judge the following:

⊙ Can you hear me? Do I speak with strength? Is it clear that I want to be heard?

⊙ Do I project a range of feelings or attitudes? When I want to sound authoritative is it heard that way? When I want to show a sense of humor does that come across? Does my voice capture your attention?

⊙ Am I pleasing to hear? Do I pitch my voice too high? Is it strong and full of body, or do I sound like a scratch on the chalkboard?

⊙ Can you "pigeonhole" me right away? Accents are often charming. To an American the sound of an Aussie voice or an Irish brogue or a South African dialect can be wonderfully attractive. But if the sound is too parochial (too much an indication that you've never left the confines of your neighborhood), you will be harder to listen to outside your own small (however important) circle.

Finding the answers to these questions is no different from asking your best friend if she likes the jacket you just tried on. You are searching for an outsider's point of view.

I know, this BIG $ecret is about self-acceptance. Why then is $ecret Four questioning your voice? Because the voice can vividly reflect whether or not you really do accept yourself. Until the inner voice is singing, the outer voice needs attention. So what if you aren't blessed with the voice of Lauren Bacall or Lauryn Hill?

⊙ **Practice.** Find a children's library that needs a volunteer to read out loud. Children are great to practice on—they give candid feedback, but the stakes aren't life and death.

⊙ **Join a drama group or the debating club.** Both groups will force you to develop your voice as though it were your most powerful instrument. It is.

⊙ **Take classes.** Whether it's a weekend course at the local learning center for "Self-Presentation" or a speech class at school, you will develop technical skill in the use of your voice.

⊙ **Listen to people whose voices you like or who grab your attention.** How do they use their voice for best effect?

⊙ **Take singing lessons.** Learn how to breathe properly to use your voice for power.

⊙ **Read poetry at a local café, or listen to others read poetry.** Notice how they use their voices, practice different effects with your own.

What It Does

This is where self-acceptance really shows itself. Every human being's worst scenarios include:

⊙ You open your mouth, say something, and all around you there is silence. You know you have said something shocking, inappropriate, or worse—stupid.

⊙ You open your mouth, say something, and everyone continues talking as though you weren't there. They do not hear you.

⊙ You open your mouth, say something you don't intend as a joke, and laughter drowns you.

These fears could legitimately inhibit the exercise of anyone's voice. But consider alternative scenarios:

- ⊙ You open your mouth, say something, and the silence that follows comes from the impact you make on the audience.

- ⊙ You say something and suddenly everyone listens with anticipation to what you will say next.

- ⊙ You say something, you may *not* intend as a joke, but its originality tickles your audience's funnybone and they laugh *with* you.

A Little Help from Your Friends

Ask your friends to catch you when you start using too many "you knows." Think of it:

Four score and, like seven years ago, you know, our foremothers, you know, upon this continent, a new nation, conceived in, uh liberty and, you know, dedicated to the proposition that, uh, uh, all women are created, like, equal.

Taken with liberty, you know, from a speech by Senator Byrd. Delivered to Congress July 10, 1998.

Voice is powerful—as a muscle it can change the world. Ever hear tapes of Eleanor Roosevelt? She actually did not have a very pleasing voice—all high and quavery. But her passion and the conviction of her beliefs allowed her to transcend the sound and reach people's hearts. What she said mattered, she believed it mattered, and she made others listen to her.

Can you listen to a recording of Martin Luther King, Jr. and not feel goosebumps? He, too, expressed with utter conviction the depth of his values, his deep belief in the overwhelming importance of universal equality and justice. What he said was fueled by how he felt about what he said, and even those who fought viciously against him, heard what he had to say.

As you accept the depth of your own feelings, and use your voice to express them, you will get attention. You may not always want it—perhaps that little pea voice is a good defense against attention. If no one can hear you, what you say doesn't really matter.

But what if you're in a situation when a hate joke is told? Or what if a decision being made in city council will affect the quality of life for certain members of the community in a way that disturbs you? Can you remain quiet? Not if you're committed to becoming an independent femme. The following situations illustrate the many uses of your voice:

> "I don't love anything more than hearing my own voice. It's a personal adoration."[1]
>
> —Leontyne Price, opera singer and first Black person to establish worldwide status as prima donna absoluta, winner of 18 Grammy's.

- ⊙ You can use your voice to articulate ideas that others haven't yet put into words.
- ⊙ You can use your voice to cause people to question foolish or harmful actions.
- ⊙ You can use your voice to inspire and move people to greatness. But it must be exercised mindfully, and the more in control of it you are—the more you know how to make it sound powerful—the more impact your voice will have. And that means taking responsibility for your inner voice—*accepting the inner voice and letting it be heard outwardly!*

When It's Used

My biggest mistakes happen when I ignore my inner voice and choose not to speak out because: (*a*) it's not the right time (I need more information, or it would be impolite); (*b*) I'm not sure if I'm alone in my view, and I don't want to test the water; or (*c*) I wait for someone else to speak out first.

It is true that silence is sometimes golden. And I do practice discretion more often now. (The advice your mother gave you

---

1. Lanker, Brian. *I Dream a World: Portraits of Black Women Who Changed America.* NY: Stewart, Chabori & Chang, 1989.

about engaging brain before putting mouth in gear really is use-ful.) But indie women do not always wait to see which way the winds are blowing before they decide to use their voices. They're the people that others wait to hear from. They set the direction of the wind.

The Lisa Simpson School of Exercising Voice calls for being the one willing to state the obvious, being the person who makes everyone else stop talking by the clarity of her thinking and her voice. (This, as opposed to the Homer Simpson School of Voice which says you NEVER bother to think before opening your mouth!) There is virtue in being mindful of others' feelings; hav-ing the sensitivity to know when exercising your voice will have the greatest impact is critical. But choosing not to exercise your voice because you are afraid or are unwilling to risk disapproval from others is not worthy of an independent femme. Think about the people who have used their voices for your well-being. So-journer Truth, Susan B. Anthony, and Gloria Steinem, to name a few. You owe it to the voices that gave you opportunity, to pass on the same gift to others.

Gear, Resources, and Actions for GETTING LOUD

Check Out These Books

Dale, Paulette. *Did You Say Something, Susan?: How Any Woman Can Gain Confidence With Assertive Communication.* New Jersey: Carol Publishing Group, 1998.

Rhodes, Lisa Renee. *Barbara Jordan: Voice of Democracy.* Danbury: Franklin Watts Inc, 1998.

Stuttard, Marie. *The Power of Speech.* Hauppauge: Barrons Educa-tional Series, 1997.

Stewart, Whitney. *Aung San Suu Kyi: Fearless Voice of Burma*. Minneapolis: Lerner Publishing Group, 1997.

Zoller, Bettye Pierce, John Arthur Watkins, Hugh Lampman, Edward Asner. *Power Talk: Standard America: Your Ladder to Success/Book and Cassettes*. Dallas: ZWL Publishing, 1994.

Try These Organizations

Storytellers School of Toronto
791 St. Clair Avenue
W. Toronto, Ontario
Canada M6C 1B7
(416) 656-2445

Toastmasters International
P.O. Box 9052
Mission Viejo, CA 92690
(949) 858-8255
www.toastmasters.org

National Forensic League
125 Watson Street
Ripon, WI 54971
(920) 748-6206

Australian Storytelling Guild (NSW) Inc.
02-9636 2727
stories@s054.aone.net.au

Visit These Web Sites

www.fray.org

www.voiceofwomen.com

See These Videos

The Joy Luck Club, 1993, based on the novel by Amy Tan.
Not For Ourselves Alone: The Story of Elizabeth Cady Stanton and Susan B. Anthony, 1999, a documentary by Ken Burns.

Try This

Let your friends fill out this questionnaire and rate your voices.

My Voice Is

    a. __ Too fast

    b. __ Too slow

    c. __ Monotonous

    d. __ Poor in phrasing, irregular rhythm of speaking

    e. __ Hesitant

    f. __ Other

    g. __ Too loud

    h. __ Too weak

    i. __ Lacking in variety

    j. __ Too forceful, unvaried

    k. __ Too high

    l. __ Too low

    m. __ Fixed, no variation

    n. __ Nasal

    o. __ Hoarse

    p. __ Breathy

    q. __ Harsh

    r. __ Shrill

    s. __ Flat

BIG $ecret Two:

Uncover Yourself

Independent femmes eat more knowledge than chocolate, are Trekkie-like in their curiosity about places (and unexplored ideas) where "no woman or man has gone before," and fiercely resist boundaries or boxes that keep them neatly packaged in OPIs (other people's ideas).

The really independent grrl is always looking behind "door number three" and willing to be found wrong in her most basic assumptions. **She delves deeper to uncover her true self.** This path is for the brave only. Living with what we know to be true, while failing to get under the rock where strange (and potentially glorious stuff) may be growing, is the coward's way.

BIG $ecret Two is to learn about the secrets of your own soul—to peel away the layers of your very being and uncover the possibilities of what you might be—by becoming a lifelong learning junkie.

Whether you explore from the intimacy of a chair in a quiet corner of your room or travel the world as Mary Polo, the imaginary sister of real-life explorer Marco, you will constantly challenge your own views of reality, of what is true about your point

> **" The learners will inherit the future, the learned will be prepared for a future that no longer "
> exists.**
> —Eric Hoffer, Bard of the Embarcadero

of view, of things you call constant, and of ideas you've held since you were barely conscious.

The four secrets in Part Two describe ways to uncover yourself. Eric Hoffer, the labor organizer and Bard of the Embarcadero (that's in San Francisco for those of you not steeped in S.F. lore) once said, "The learners will inherit the future, the learned will be prepared for a future that no longer exists."

He meant that people who just accept what is, without constantly questioning, testing, and uncovering, will be obsolete before their time—prepared for a world in which their knowledge is already old. Indie women don't allow this to happen.

Rock and Read

"Being 'ignorant' is just not knowing stuff yet. Being stupid is staying ignorant about important stuff when you have the choice to become informed."
—Derrenda Perry

The American Booksellers Association sponsors a Banned Books Week annually. They want to remind us that it wasn't just in Germany under Hitler or Chile under Pinochet that the right to read freely was restricted—but that every day, sometimes in our own hometowns, people make decisions about what ideas and information we should be exposed to.

- *Forever* by Judy Blume was removed from the Frost Junior High School Library in 1993 because "it's basically a sexual how-to book for junior high students."

- *The Autobiography of Malcolm X* was restricted at the Jacksonville, Florida, middle school libraries because "it presents a racist view of white people and is a 'how-to manual' for crime."

- ◉ *The Handmaid's Tale* by Margaret Atwood was removed from the Chicopee Falls, Massachusetts, high school English reading list in 1993 because it "contains profanity and sex."

- ◉ *Harry Potter and the Sorcerer's Stone* by J. K. Rowling, has been removed from school districts all over the United States because of "the book's advocacy of witchcraft."

Books that are banned—or "restricted"—are books that someone else thinks you're not supposed to read. If you did read them, you might develop ideas of your own—contrary ideas. Feelings, thoughts, emotions, knowledge. Independent women know that reading controversial books is essential to maintaining a free head. So go ahead, stay tuned to Banned Books on-line (**www.cs.cmu.edu/people/spok/banned-books.html**), read banned books, and fight for your right to do so. Rock and read.

Text of the First Amendment

Congress shall make no law respecting an establishment of religion, or prohibiting the free exercise thereof; or abridging the freedom of speech, or of the press; or the right of the people peaceably to assemble, and to petition the Government for a redress of grievances.

Don't Limit Yourself

Independent women, financially savvy people, and those who seem to be "lucky" more often than others, also read. It's their edge. They always know a bit more than the next person; they are always a little more prepared, more tuned in.

The Little Engine That Could. Nancy Drew. Cossette. Collette. Wonder Woman. Frida Kahlo. Time travel. Dinosaurs. Teleportation. Easter Island. I am a collage of the people and places and ideas I've discovered in books that have helped shape my dreams. Vision expands when we read about people and places that can inspire our own thoughts and ideas. Possibility grows.

I used to ask femmes what kind of business they might imagine themselves owning. The frequency of the response "nail

salon" was alarming. If occasionally I had even heard that someone wanted a chain of nail salons, or maybe the first nail salon to
open on Mars, I might have felt better. But what I heard was an
appalling smallness of possibility that would have real consequences for life. "If I can't dream it I can't be it," to misquote
Sojourner Truth. Reading expands dreams. ***Dreams expand possibility and reading is the food of dreams.***

It is a commonly held stereotype that the wired generation
doesn't read. The prevailing bias is that television and computers
have so addled the brains of Generation D that the ability, indeed
the joy, of reading has been lost.

But every time I read another report on the deteriorating reading habits of the Millenium Generation, I think of Lelah Baker
Rabe who was 40 when she was 14 and who had read more
of Shakespeare by the age of 16 than I have yet. I think of 20-
something Victoria Groves, whose reading and knowledge far
surpasses that of many older adults.

So I have a somewhat different perspective on what is being
read among the so-called illiterate cyber-generation. Nevertheless, while you can overeat, you can't overread. And what one
reads generally and what one reads with the express purpose of
developing true independence may be different.

Reading Checklist

Check any of the following you have read in the last three
months:

___ The business and news sections of your local newspaper
___ Any business publication (*The Wall Street Journal, Working
Woman, Fast Company, Wired, Inc., The Economist*)
___ A "how-to" or instructional book on a subject that in-
terests you
___ Any specialty magazine having to do with a cause or
issue you care about
___ The op-ed section of any newspaper

__ Any magazine that covers subjects other than fashion or celebrities

__ Any international publication

__ A novel or biography

Name any cybersites you have visited in the last three months:

_____

_____

_____

Now check any of the following you have read in the last four weeks:

__ Any fashion magazine

__ Any celebrity-focused magazine

__ Any magazine for girls or women

__ Dilbert cartoons

What did you find? The point of this exercise is not to make you feel inadequate (you aren't), but to point out the habits that shape your reading life. Independent women expand their boundaries. They work, think, and READ. They are well aware of what's going on around them, what's happening, what's up. They sense new trends, not only because they have strong inner voices that they listen to, but because they stay informed when they read.

I drive the people I work with crazy. I start way too many sentences with, "Have you read—?" But they know I usually have some piece of information, a bit of the puzzle that may give us the additional knowledge we need to make our company special, invent a new product, understand an emerging need in the world.

Expand Your Reading Repertoire

Here's a way to develop your reading habits to support your quest for independence. Create five labels: Great Thoughts, Contemporary Knowledge, Expertise, Pop Culture, and Fun. Place them at different spots around the room.

Great Thoughts

Look around your house, dorm room, or apartment and see which books you have that explore life's great questions: life and death, love and loss, discovery and possibility. (Don't forget books you borrowed from the library or a friend; write their titles on slips of paper and stick them like placeholders in the right categories.) You might have works by great writers, a copy of the Bible or the Koran, the teachings of the Dalai Lama, biographies of Renaissance or Impressionist artists, the history of Pompeii, or the letters of Virginia Woolf. This is classic literature; you may have had it on your high school or college reading lists, or read it because you were curious about the meaning of life. Independent people are drawn to explore life's extraordinary questions of meaning and hope and despair. Put those books near the GREAT THOUGHTS label.

Contemporary Knowledge

Now find books or magazines that speak to business, science, and politics. These are the books that inform you of pressing trends, things that will affect the world and your place in it. Maybe you read *Sky & Telescope, Fast Company,* or *Scientific American* magazine. Or maybe you have a book by Stephen Jay Gould or a biography of Anita Roddick. (Who are they? you ask. Amazon.com was invented for you.)

Independent women KNOW stuff. They don't remember every fact they've ever read, but they do put together the ideas they read and try to make sense of how they all fit together. What does a drought in Korea have to do with starving children and what does that have to do with the interest paid on your savings account in your local bank? What does the burning of trees in the Amazon have to do with the cost of that new desk you want for your bedroom? How does the cloning of Dolly the Sheep have anything to do with a visit to your doctor? What does the election of a corrupt politician have to do with the education of children in the inner cities?

Independent thinkers have answers to these questions, and they have answers because they read and think about where they stand on the issues. They don't allow others to tell them where to stand. Place these books near the label CONTEMPORARY KNOWLEDGE.

Expertise

What are you especially interested in? Whether you collect stamps or aspire to be a concert flutist, whether you have aspirations to be the next Martha Stewart or to build bridges on Mars, you have to develop deep knowledge that includes history, biography, reports, trends, and technical knowledge. Place any books or magazines that support your developing knowledge of your interests near the label EXPERTISE.

Pop Culture

Now fill the shelf marked POP CULTURE with the books and magazines in your house that reveal hip new trends. Maybe for you it's *Jane* or *People* magazine, or *Soap Opera Digest*. Maybe it's *Time* or *Life* magazines, or the latest celebrity bio.

Snobs consider this stuff junk, but these magazines indicate what's going on in society's psyche. You knew before the rest of the world that a rave was a party, and that DiCaprio was not a latte. You knew because you're pop culture literate.

Pop culture is full of icons and omens. Understanding where the popular culture is and the ways in which you want (or don't want) to be part of it, gives you the knowledge and ability to choose your place in the culture rather than be ruled by it. Only an idiot follows trends and fads slavishly. Independents set their own path; they understand the culture and make choices about how and when to participate in it—or not.

Fun

Now place the things you read for pure *fun* beside that label. Do you read science fiction? Astrology guides? Anything Sue Grafton or Terry MacMillan writes? Whatever gives you a kick, add to this pile.

As a kid, I used my fun reading as a means of escape. Sometimes it was also a convenient way to block out the world, ignore things I didn't want to deal with—and sometimes that's still true for me. I watch myself. When my fun pile is higher than any of my other piles, it's a clue that maybe there's something happening in my life that I don't want to deal with—then it's time to put aside the book and do some reflecting (see $ecret 19!).

Indie grrls use their brains; they don't hide from things. On the other hand, they know that fun is good for the soul and thus don't deprive themselves. (It's like chocolate. Eat the whole box and you're foolish; eat one really exquisite piece and you're discriminating.)

Take Stock of the Stacks

So how does it look? Are your stacks pretty well balanced? Or do you have a tall pile in one category and none in some categories? Is your recreation pile full but your great questions pile flat? Ask independent women what they read that has meaning to them. The women I know all read different things, but they have the following in common:

1. Deep curiosity (driven by the need to know)
2. Passion (fed by knowledge)

3. Authority (people listen to them)
4. A sense of humor (that comes from understanding many perspectives)
5. Sophistication (a result of worldly knowledge)

Does knowing what Oprah reads make you want to read the same book? I have friends with whom I regularly share book titles. One of my male buddies can always be counted on for the name of a great new mystery or an author I might not have discovered yet. The head of a design foundation keeps me in touch with cutting edge books about design and designers; a friend of mine who is also a writer is a great source of books written about women. Whenever possible, I ask fun and interesting people to tell me what they are currently reading—that gives me windows into worlds I might never explore otherwise.

10 Ways to Make Reading Rock

Regardless of what we each read, there are ways to expand our literary world. Using any or all of the following methods will broaden the scope of your reading life, increase your knowledge, and expand your gray matter.

1. Fish in a Magazine Stand (as well as on-line)

Every few months, try two to five magazines or web sites in areas you wouldn't normally read. Pick up a magazine on astronomy, stamp collecting, or sports that you haven't read before. Or read *Numismatics, Car Racing, Jet, Civilization, Latina, Jane, Money Magazine,* or *Outside.* (This doesn't have to be expensive—visit the library for a free fishing expedition—or check out the on-line versions of these periodicals.)

This trick is how really *savvy* people (and professional futurists—now there's a career choice to explore) "scan the environment." They delve into unfamiliar territory searching for clues and patterns that give them insight into what's coming around the bend. And you never know, you just might open a window to an adventure you can't even imagine.

2. Launch a Reading Group

Oprah's Book Club has had a phenomenal impact on getting people reading and talking together. Reading groups are small groups of people who meet one or two times a month to discuss books they read together. It's a great way to explore many points of view, and get more out of a book. (Pull together a group of friends to discuss the $ecrets in this book, for example.)

3. Turn Off the Tube, and Read a Book

I try not to miss *Ally McBeal* and *ER;* I love movies and videos. But I devote the late night hours to reading before bed. Choose your time—maybe you're a morning reader or perhaps you can only steal those 20 minutes when you usually take over the bathroom. Whatever your pleasure, make sure your reading space feels like a snug spot, a secret garden—a place to disappear, Ray Bradbury–like, into the pages of another world.

4. Write All Over the Margins and Between the Lines in Your Books and Magazines

The philosopher Mortimer Adler wrote *How to Read a Book*. I remember thinking it seemed like a stupid idea for a book, but since I had enjoyed other things he'd written, I took a leap of faith and read the book. (You do this with writers whom you get to know—you cut them some slack because they have given you good hours and you owe them.)

The man set me free. He gave me permission to write in my books. "Write notes in the margins," he said. "Argue with the author, underline things you want to remember or check on later." At first I felt really guilty—all through school I had been warned

NEVER to write in my books; it was cause for demerits or something worse. Now here was an extremely educated man telling me to write in books?!

It was great advice. Ever since I began to use my books as living friends, I find I treat them differently. Writing in a book makes it uniquely mine. I add my thoughts, questions, and feelings as though in a journal. I can do more research, remember a point I want to share with a friend, or find another book that argues with an idea I question. Books become more vibrant when you treat them like intellectual companions. (Note: If you're reading a rare first edition, you may want to think twice about this—or pick up a less valuable copy of the same book at a second-hand bookstore!)

5. Read Your Enemies

Think of it as liver for the soul—it's good for you. Be sure you read people who disagree with you as well as those with whom you violently agree. You often learn more from those whose points of view you do not share than from those you do.

For example, I'm a sworn enemy of Rush Limbaugh. The man seems to contradict every bloody value I hold dear. But if I ignore him and do not read his books or listen to what he has to say, I'm just as ignorant as he is. So read your enemies.

6. Be an Activist Reader

Tear out articles and circulate them among friends. Send copies of books that make a point to someone you are in conversation with. Have you read an op-ed piece you think is terrific? Did you read an article that explodes current comfortable ideas? If you want to shake up your friends, introduce an uncomfortable subject in the family, or just start a conversation with someone you care about, share the article or book and get people talking.

Question everything you read. Who wrote it? What was the writer's agenda? Who has written something else that supports this writer? Who disagrees with the writer? Reading is one signif-

How to Rock and Read
1. Fish in a magazine stand.
2. Launch a reading group.
3. Turn off the tube.
4. Write in the margins.
5. Be an activist reader.
6. Read your enemies.
7. Frequent independent and offbeat bookstores.
8. Use audiobooks.
9. Read banned books.
10. Keep a book journal.

icant way to collect knowledge and wisdom. But just because something is in print doesn't mean it's true. Question authors!

7. Frequent Independent and Offbeat Bookstores

Barnes & Noble is a great resource for mainstream reading. But the serious reader doesn't follow only the mainstream any more than the serious music buff sticks to the Top 40. To ferret out great books you sometimes need to wander off the beaten path.

In my small town, there's a used bookstore called Bart's. At Bart's Bookstore I can find a book in the middle of the night if I feel the urge. Bart has books lined up on shelves along the outer wall of the store and I can put the cost of the book in a slot in the door (wacky, but it works!). He also carries first editions and a great collection of used books about the history of Hollywood as well as books on California wildflowers. There is always a treasure for me in this bookstore—and usually at a price way below what I would have to pay for a new book in the local chain.

There are bookstores that specialize in mysteries (The Phantom Bookstore in Ventura, California, for example, is a great source for books by Erle Stanley Gardner, the author of the Perry Mason mysteries. Gardner lived in Ventura, hence the deep knowledge and interest in his work); some stores sell only books on food and cooking; others carry only travel books. And the owner of a good independent bookstore—like Ed Elrod of The Ojai Table of Contents—is more than a bookseller, he is a guide to other worlds. I can ask Ed *anything* and he'll lead me to a book I have never heard of and set my world on its ears.

A true book lover searches for bookstores the way wine lovers seek out great vineyards. Traveling in new cities I always look for independent bookstores for useful information about the new place I'm visiting and to find whatever quirky collections it has in store.

8. Substitute Audio Books for Paula Cole and 'NSync

Do you use a Walkman when you ride a bike or jog or work out?

Try audio books as an alternate with your favorite tunes. Remember how comforting it was as a kid to have stories read to you? Take advantage of the new technology and be entertained by storytellers again while you exercise or travel. You can borrow them from your local library for free.

9. Read Banned Books

You have a responsibility to the First Amendment to battle those forces who want to close down your ability to read and think for yourself. Reading a banned book is one way an independent person can stand up and be counted.

10. Keep a Book Journal

I didn't start this until recently and now I can't recommend all the books I have loved over the years. Create a journal form of your own or use the form in the "Gear" Section to keep track. You will find that your journal will reveal a lot about who you are, what your interests have been, and what is important to you. It's a great way to do an annual inventory of who you are and where you are going!

Gear, Resources and Actions for Rocking and Reading

Check Out These Books

Adler, Mortimer. *How to Read a Book*. New York: Simon and Schuster, 1972.

Foerstal, Herbert. *Banned Media in the USA; A Reference Guide to Censorship in the Press, Motion Pictures, Broadcasting and the Internet*. Westport: Greenwood Publishing, 1998.

Quinlan, Anna. *How Reading Changed My Life (Library of Contemporary Thought)*. New York: Ballantine Books, 1998.

Try These Organizations

Great Books Foundation

35 E. Wacker Drive

Suite 2300

Chicago, IL 60601

(800) 222-5870

www.greatbooks.com

Visit These Web Sites

www.amazon.com

www.booksatoz.com

www.freeexpression.com

www.fatbrain.com

Try This

Copy this and create your own book journal.

	Great Questions	Contemporary Knowledge	Expertise	Pop Culture	Fun
Title	☐	☐	☐	☐	☐
Author					
Date Read Comments:					

$ecret 6

Explore!

" Work like you don't need the money, dance like no one's watch-ing, and love like you've never been hurt!.
—Megan Acedo

The world is a dangerous place. We've learned to be as wary as a dog smelling a porcupine. We are warned to be careful—not to be out alone after dark, to guard our purses, and to walk with confidence down an empty street. We march to "take back the night," buy Mace for protection, sign up for courses in self-defense, and travel in packs. With so many danger signals echoing through the culture, it's easy to see how our world can be made smaller, bound as it is in caution and apprehension.

What's a girl to do? Hang out in well-lit malls and stay close to home? Date only bodybuilders and take them everywhere we go? Wear flak jackets under our Gap denims? I don't think so. Independent grrls make tracks. They spend less time in malls and more time "where the wild things are." They are on the offensive—not the defensive. They are independent because they are AT HOME in the world, not frightened of it.

But how do you explore the world without being reckless or putting yourself at unnecessary risk? Indie grrls aren't stupid. I don't hike deep canyons alone, and I don't walk lonely streets at night in cities where I am not "at home." I lock my doors, tell people where I am going to be, and I never flash cash on the street or in a store. (And I write "See Photo ID" on the backs of all my credit cards—so if someone *does* steal my wallet, they can't so easily steal my credit.) Evil abounds. I pay attention. But I do explore, as do some of the most intriguing people the world knows.

The Explorers Club was founded in 1904. In describing their criteria for membership, the club brochure states:

> *The tourist* may travel widely, singly, or with a group, and more often than not will be guided over previously traveled routes, even if remote, primarily for the purposes of pleasure and attainment of self-knowledge or education. *The explorer* or field scientist, on the other hand, explores an unknown or little known region and/or area of science to gain new knowledge for humankind.

In other words, if you travel independently, over new ground, you are a true explorer. Of course it wasn't until 1981 that the Explorers Club allowed women to join their little society, but that doesn't mean women were not taking off for parts unknown.

And though I expect many readers one day to qualify for Explorers Club membership, you don't need to climb a virgin peak, journey to the subterranean caves of Turkey, or be the first to step on Mars (though some of you will) to qualify as an independent woman. But there are ways of getting comfortable outside mall walls and beyond the intimate cluster of people who already know you. Here are a few goals to tackle.

Explore Your Town—Know It Better Than Anyone

Whether you live in a town of under 10,000 or over 1,000,000, you live in a small universe with opportunities for adventure and independence. Spend a year, or a summer, or a series of week ends getting to know your town in the same way a tourist might.

Call the Chamber of Commerce and ask for their list of "points of interest" that's usually given to tourists. See anything on that list you haven't checked out already? Make a date to visit, take a friend, and explore the destination together. Or maybe you have a tourist board in town. Get their list of the strangest, tackiest things a tourist might do—find out what the attraction is.

On a business trip to Rochester, New York, I visited the home of Susan B. Anthony, one of my heroines. If you live in Rochester and haven't visited her house, you've missed a great treasure. On the road in California, I make a point of visiting the old missions that tell the story of the state's history.

Regardless of where you live, there are gems to be uncovered and polished. I live in a town with a population of 7,500. After ten years here, I'm still a relative newcomer. But I give as good a tour of this little village as any professional guide. Taking my friends around, telling stories of local history makers, and giving them something other than a walk down Main Street puts me in the driver's seat. I'm an authority, an expert—I can lead, not just follow. And people like to visit me because they know I have good stories, rare information—a visit to my sleepy town will be anything but quiet!

Travel

Regardless of your age you can explore the world in ways that do not necessarily cost a fortune or require you to sign away your life in servitude as a nanny or a sailor—though those options are just right for some people.

If you are in school—from elementary to graduate school—there are always exchange possibilities. (See "Gear, Resources, and Actions" for contacts):

You don't like the idea of an exchange program or being away for more than a month? Look up some long lost relatives and arrange an in-family exchange program. Maybe you and a cousin can swap homes for a weekend or a summer or a school semester.

Or you're feeling *really* adventurous? The Peace Corps and the Armed Services both offer subsidized travel. And for the truly industrious, fellowships are an option. The Kellogg National Fellowship Program annually gives 50 people under 30 a chance to travel and learn—whatever their hearts desire. You just have to apply. A list of opportunities is listed under "Gear, Resources, and Actions" at the end of this chapter. Check into them.

Surf the Web

There are plenty of real horror stories of girls attacked by men who stalk them after connecting in chat rooms and through various Web sites. With all due respect to Tom Hanks and Meg Ryan, *You've Got Mail* IS JUST A MOVIE.

Looking for love on the Net is a gamble I personally wouldn't make; but I have traveled extensively through Australia, Italy, and the state of Maine via the Web. I've discovered quirky sites run by individuals who introduce me to the clubs of Melbourne and the fashions of Milan. You can raise your W.Q. (Worldliness

Quotient) without ever leaving your room, and you are more in-dependent for having access to information others have not both-ered to collect.

Lead

What would you really love to do but think is impossible? Where in the world do you want to go? You can go anywhere and do anything, but you'll have to take charge to do it. Age is not an issue, but degree of determination is. If you want to be a woman of the world, you have to explore, and sometimes that means leading the way. Here are four expeditions you can lead. I have listed them in order of difficulty. Start with the first and work your way up and soon you'll be Explorers Club material—or at least ready for the DollarDiva's Club.

Organize a Hike

Whether you live in Brooklyn, New York, the Ozark Mountains of Missouri, the Swiss Alps, or the suburbs of Melbourne, Aus-tralia, there are hiking trails within a short distance of your home. A great resource for locating those trails is a publishing company in Birmingham, Alabama, called Menasha Ridge Press.

Menasha Ridge specializes in books on travel and adventure around the world. Call (800) 558-7078 and ask for their catalog. Or visit your local library. You may hike the park lanes of a major city or the foothill trails in a forest grove. One of the most strenu-ous 10K hikes I've ever taken winds through Tuscan foothills to a ninth-century abbey. Adventure is often in your own backyard, but exploring that backyard is something that only the intrepid woman undertakes.

Once you've settled on your destination, decide who you will take with you. Friends you know? Or is this a chance to add some new people to your PDA? Maybe each friend brings a friend. Whichever way you go, send out the invitations, set a time, make sure everyone packs his or her own sandwich, and set a place to meet. Maybe you'll require everyone to bring an exotic cookie for a mid-hike cookie swap. I have a friend with whom I hike, and we've grown pretty sophisticated about trying new trail mixes. (So far the pistachio, sunflower seed, and raisin mix tops our list!)

You can make this a more interesting expedition if you've done your homework. Can you put together a cassette with stories about the area in which you will be hiking? How about giving a few of the hikers a wildflowers guide, handing a bird guide to others, and a tree guide to the rest—then make sure everyone shares what they see, hear, or discover. Or ask everyone to bring a favorite poem to share along the way. Your job as the expedition leader is to LEAD, inspire, and help others discover. Believe me, independent women are at the head of the pack, not straggling at the rear.

Organize a Group Trip

Now you have to get more resourceful—and more daring. Pick a place that has an entrance fee. You're going to figure out how to get yourself in for nothing.

You can call and find out if they have group rates. Sometimes the site will make an arrangement that if you get, say, 10 visitors, you get in free. If they don't offer, ask for it.

If they won't agree to this, collect the fees and add enough to cover your own costs. Remember this is a practice run for you—you are working on how to lead, explore, and travel for nothing. So as an example, let's say you're going to take a group of friends to the Metreon in San Francisco, the opera in Sydney, or to a play your local theater company is presenting. What value can you add to the experience to make it worthwhile for your friends to pay a premium price for you to be the organizer?

How about picking everyone up in a limo? (Or getting them there on the bus and having the limo make the home trip.) What about adding an elegant picnic to the event? (Remember: be sure you make a profit out of this.) Or can the place you are visiting

"I would drive to Bocco di Falco, a straggling dirty village . . . and spend the long hours of those sweet summer days hunting the Pherusa, a wild, wind-blown creature who would often lead me along an arduous chase over the loose stones and tangled herbage . . ."

—Margaret Fountaine, describing her hunt for wild butterflies in Italy in the late 1870s.[1]

arrange a VIP tour for you? A visit backstage with the cast of the play or a look at how IMAX really works might be worth the extra price of the ticket.

Organizing a group trip is a little like herding cats and is a true test of leadership. If you can get everyone to your destination on time, see that they have a good time, and get them home with you still sane, you've succeeded. And you now have the experience you need to raise the stakes and try your leadership skills at another level of complexity!

Organize a Trip to a Sporting Event, a Concert, or a Political Event in Another State

Are you ready to try a river rafting trip for a group of friends? Do you wonder what it would be like to attend a political convention? Take the lessons you've learned from your previous expeditions, and hit the road. The principles are always the same:

1. *Do the homework.* Make the calls, send for the information, check the Web for background info.
2. *Figure out all costs and logistics.* How will you get there? What will all the expenses be? What will you need to charge others to subsidize your role as the leader?
3. *Work out the creative details of the trip.* That is, what are the elements you can create that make this a special trip—one more memorable than if your sister travelers went on their own?
4. *Communicate the opportunity.* Market the idea! E-mail the idea to people you think might make great traveling companions. Send letters describing the day, add details to show how organized you already are. This will give your potential clients/sister travelers comfort that they are in good hands.

---

1. Morris Mary, ed. *Maiden Voyages: Writings of Women Travelers,* NY: Vintage Books, 1993.

5. *Make checklists* for every possible contingency, and check everything twice.
6. *HAVE FUN!!* If you aren't having fun, you're doing something wrong.

Organize an International Adventure

Now you're getting serious. Find a world map and gaze at it for a while. (Make sure it was drawn in the last few years—boundaries on some continents changed pretty radically in the last century.) What part of the world calls you? What do you know about the Galápagos? Tierra del Fuego? Iceland? How about a pilgrimage to India? A summer in Spain? A dig in Greece or a trip to the Atacama Desert?

Independent people practice living outside their comfort zone. They don't just travel to familiar places where people speak their language and look like them, they travel to places that will expand their vision, open their hearts, and challenge their truths.

But international travel *is* serious business and may be easier and more fun if done in partnership with someone else. Particularly if your partner in this venture has traveled before, you'll have the added benefit of some great experience. (Remember, being independent doesn't mean always doing everything alone, it means doing new things in smart ways—organizing an international trip with an experienced traveler/co-leader is just as smart.)

The homework you need to do for an international trip is more ambitious than the preparation you did for jaunts closer to home. What are the health risks in the country? Do you need a passport? Special visas? What's the political climate of the country? Do you have local contacts? What's the weather like during the season in which you plan to travel?

"... Everyone knows that a donkey should go faster than a camel ... But this unspeakable Robin [the name she gave her donkey] knew that he had but to droop his ears and look pathetic, pause knock-kneed before a boulder perfectly easy to circumvent—his master's heart went out to him [and] ... I would be asked to walk."

—**Freya Stark, describing her winter in Arabia.**[2]

2. Ibid.

Don't know a hostel from being taken hostage? Time to learn. Staying in a private home in Jamaica is a lot different from booking into a fancy resort where you connect only with other tourists.

What's your goal for this trip? Are you thinking of studying art in Florence and want to see what living there might be like? Or are you interested in learning more about the rain forests in Costa Rica because the study of the rain forest ecology appeals to you? Are you just curious about whether or not Paris really is romantic or the outback of Australia really wild?

Be clear about why you are visiting your chosen destination. It will make all the difference in how you plan and prepare for your international adventure.

Of course, there are ways to explore without ever leaving the house. Recently I went to Martha's Vineyard, flying through the pages of *The Martha's Vineyard Cookbook* (written in 1971, it's a first edition I picked up in a recent tour of Bart's) while sitting in my bed. Cookbooks are a terrific way of exploring a country—they provide so many clues about what is important to people, what is grown locally, and what makes people feel a part of their community.

And I gazed over Tuscan hills before ever leaving the airport while reading *Under the Tuscan Sun,* by Frances Mayes. The author lives in Tuscany part of the year, and her description of daily life is so vivid that by the time I finally did get there it felt like a second trip—a return to someplace familiar.

Before I went to Rome last time, I traveled through time with a book called *Walks in Rome,* published in 1909. In the introduction the author wrote

> An arrival in Rome is very different from that in any other town in Europe. It is coming to a place new and yet familiar, strange and yet so well known . . . when they [the travelers] go to the Coliseum, it is an object whose appearance has been familiar to them from childhood. . . .

> "My main aim in going to Congo Francais was to get up above the tide line of the Ogawe River and there collect fishes; for my object on this voyage was to collect fish from a river north of the Congo."
>
> —**Mary Kingsley, writing in her journal, 1893.**[3]

3. Ibid.

Almost a century later, his words still ring true for most of us—and it is a true form of time travel to discover the walks people took in Rome a hundred years ago and then to retrace them in our own time.

You can travel through literature. (Go with Henry James on *A Little Tour in France* or hike vicariously with John Muir through his *Summer in the Sierras*.) Or travel through the letters of independent women who DID leave the house for parts unknown. Even a night spent listening to world music is a form of exploration that transcends borders and needs no passports.

Explorers and lifelong travelers often come to realize the imperative of speaking multiple languages and having friendships that cross cultures and frontiers. These people have broad perspectives and wide horizons. The opportunities available to them are simply more plentiful than if they had never left their own backyards.

Gear, Resources, and Actions for Exploring

Check Out These Books

Aebi, Tania. *Maiden Voyage*. New York: Simon & Schuster, 1989.

Blum, Arlene. *Annapurna: A Woman's Place*. San Francisco: Sierra Club Books, 1980.

Davidson, Robyn. *Tracks: A Woman's Solo Trek Across 1,700 Miles of Australian Outback*. New York: Vintage Books, 1995.

Miller, Luree. *On Top of the World: Five Women Explorers in Tibet*. Seattle: Mountaineers Books, 1984.

Olds, Elizabeth Fagg. *Women of the Four Winds*. Boston: Houghton Mifflin, 1985.

"When you go from Arequipa to Islay you have the sun behind you and the wind in front, so you suffer far less from the heat than you do when going from Islay to Arequipa. I stood up to the journey very well; besides my health had improved and I felt better able to endure its rigours this time."

—Flora Tristan, 1833, writing about a trip she took alone in Peru to stake a claim to her family's fortune.[4]

---

4. Ibid.

Simony, Maggie, Editor. *The Traveler's Reading Guide: Ready-Made Reading Lists for the Armchair Traveler.* New York: Facts on File Publications, 1993.

Tuttle, Cameron. *The Bad Girl's Guide to the Open Road.* San Francisco: Chronicle Books, 1999.

Stacy Stuart, World Traveler

By the time Stacy Stuart was a high school senior, she was well aware that she had traveled far more than her parents—who support her desire to "see the world." And she's a smart traveler. She thinks ahead to make her travel plans financially possible. She spent months before a trip with the Close-Up Club to Washington, D.C., from her home in San Jose, California, fundraising by selling candles and organizing car washes and bowl-a-thons. She now says all that hard labor was worth it as she learned more about history and government in one week in D.C. than in three years of high school social studies classes!

Stacy also spent 10 days in Italy and Greece with the Travel Club from her school. To make this trip possible, the club raised money for two years with schoolwide candy sales. Club members also worked individually to support their own expenses. Tracy went to Rome, Florence, Capri, Sorrento, Delphi, and Athens on this trip. (One of her best memories is of the Blue Grotto in the island of Capri.) As of the printing of this book, Stacy is already working on plans for her next trip. She was debating whether to go to Mexico with her high school's Travel Club, or to Hawaii with her friends after graduation. In the summer, she works at a local swimming pool to save money for either possibility.

Stacy credits her experience at Camp $tart-Up for giving her the confidence and the skills she needed to make her travel possible. That summer she learned a lot about saving money and thinking ahead; now she consciously makes the effort required to get her—literally—where she wants to go, planning, saving, and working hard. She was also motivated by meeting businesswomen who also knew what they wanted and went for it. Stacy's convinced that travel has helped her to grow as a person. She has had many new experiences and gained knowledge of the world—as well as confidence in herself.

Try These Organizations

The Council on International Travel and Exchange, New York (800) 226-8624

American Friends Service Committee Youth Programs, (215) 241-7295

Council Travel's Work Abroad Program (888) COUNCIL

People to People, overseas internships
(816) 531-4701

Australian Trust for Conservation
011 61 3 5333 1483

Willing Workers on Organic Farms (WWOOF)
(250) 354-4417 Canada

Restoration of Medieval Buildings
France
011 33 88 3717 20

World Teach
(800) 4 TEACH 0

Earthwatch Institute
(800) 776-0188

Peace Corps
(800) 424-8580
www.peacecorps.gov

Up With People
(800) 596-7353
www.upwithpeople.org

New World Teachers—"Travel the World Teaching English,"
(800) 644-5424

STA Travel—"Because Education and Travel Are Not Exclusive,"
(800) 777-0112

Visit These Web Sites
www.sta-travel.com

www.bpbasecamp.com

www.americanhiking.org

www.jasonfoundation.org

www.counciltravel.com

www.ciee.org The Council on International Travel and Exchange

Browse Through These Magazines
Student Travels, the magazine for international travel, study, and work. Published by The Council on International Travel and Exchange, New York Council Travel's Work Abroad Program (888) COUNCIL
Conde Nast's *Traveler Magazine*
Travel & Leisure

Try This
Keep a travel journal of all your trips, near and far. Review your entries occasionally and observe your habits.

\$ecret 7

Get Out of the Box

> "Living encased in a glass box is cool if you're into watching everyone around you experience life."
> —Morgan Montgomery

Outside the box is to the independent diva what skiing off-trail is to the extreme athlete. Outside the box isn't for everyone, but for the indie soul, it's the only place to be. Outside the box is where the action is—there are no worn paths, no rigid rules to follow, no clear boundaries to hem you in. Outside the box is where YOU PURSUE YOUR PASSION. It's where

- ⊙ creative thought flourishes,
- ⊙ surprise reigns, and
- ⊙ discovery and action merge.

The independent femme climbs outside the box because that's where she has the greatest amount of freedom. To think and act outside the box is to be creative. Consider these "Ah hah!" experiences:

- ◉ At Camp $tart-Up a couple of years ago, Annie Taylor and her team came up with an idea for a surfboard designed for women because, "No one has ever designed a surfboard for women that is short enough and light enough to fit their different bodies." They called their company WaterLily™ and plan to market to surfer girls. Ah hah! Why didn't I think of that?

- ◉ Fifteen-year-old Meghan Elganter raised goats as part of her 4-H responsibility. But she thought that blue ribbons weren't quite enough so she figured out how to turn the goat milk into body lotion and sells it as a beauty product. Ah hah! Why didn't I think of that?

- ◉ Allison Beckwith created a Web site for selling hip products to the anything-but-average Christian teen (**www.flare.com**). Ah hah! Why didn't I think of that?

- ◉ At 16, Heisi Figeroa was already an Avon Lady in her East Boston neighborhood. But many of her clients spoke and read only Spanish. When she couldn't get Spanish language catalogs from the big company, she translated them herself for her clients and sales boomed! Ah hah! Why didn't Avon think of that?!!

Why do some people think only inside the box—that is, in ordinary ways—and others find solutions that are more imaginative? ***Independent thinkers rarely accept what is as what must be***. You can identify an independent thinker by the number of times you hear her say, "What if . . ." or "Why not?"

Something Different *Is* Possible

Accepting the status quo when it no longer works shows a lack of imagination. Are you ever called stubborn? Maybe someone tagged you in a more positive way than they realized. Stubborn can be another word for tenacious or independent. Stubborn people may simply be mulish, but a stubborn person may also be someone who is dissatisfied with the way things are and convinced that something different is possible.

In 1980, Edwin Land, the inventor of Polaroid instant film, wrote a letter to the shareholders of his company. Describing what he felt to be the secret for a great future, he wrote, "Do not undertake the program unless the goal is manifestly important and nearly impossible; do not do anything that anyone else can do readily." Indeed, that is how instant film came to life.

One day in the sixties, in Albuquerque, New Mexico, he was having lunch with his family when someone at the table took a picture of the gathering. His daughter turned to him and asked, "Why can't I see the picture now, Daddy?" Why not? he wondered, and spent the next couple of decades answering that question. Instant photography broke what was considered the "laws" of physics.

> "Do not under-take the program unless the goal is manifestly important and nearly impossible; do not do anything that anyone else can do readily."
> —Edwin Land, inventor

Land spent decades of his life studying the properties of light and chemicals that would create a picture that developed instantly, giving his daughter what she wanted: a picture, now. Those years, he felt, were spent in a way that gave meaning and excitement to his life—in spite of the number of failures he experienced along the way, or the number of people who thought he was a little eccentric for pursuing his passion with such fervor.

But he was having fun! He woke up every morning prepared to challenge conventional wisdom and rules, refusing to accept that the impossible was impossible. And today—almost a half century after his daughter posed the "Why not, Daddy?" Polaroid offers sticky back photos to Y-Gens who want to use photography as a tool of collage. The I-Zone camera opened up a whole new "out of the box" experience for photography buffs.

People who are in the habit of saying, "It can't be done," or "That will never work," are rarely outside-the-box thinkers. To believe you can have success when everyone around you has failed or has given up on finding a solution to a vexing problem is to be either a little lunatic or a great deal optimistic. Or maybe it is simply the normal 'tude of the independent thinker, willing to follow her own ideas and intuitions, making her own mistakes and discoveries.

Get Complex

Professor Mihaly Csikszentmihalyi, author of *Creativity: Flow and the Psychology of Discovery and Invention,* suggests that the single common trait among rule-breaking thinkers is their complexity. Complex people hold contradictory thoughts and actions. (And you just thought you were crazy.) For example, most people are both aggressive and cooperative, but one quality is more highly developed than the other. Complex people on the other hand, may demonstrate both qualities, either at the same time, or different times, depending on the circumstances.

Do you confuse your friends and family? Are coworkers puzzled by your actions and points of view? GREAT! All good signs of complexity! Outside-the-box thinkers don't always please those around them. When everyone thinks alike, and life rolls smoothly along, to have an independent spirit rock the boat, raise a hard question, or go off on a tangent can be annoying. "There she goes again," I became used to hearing.

Over time, I came to appreciate that I was on to something good as soon as the people around me were uncomfortable. But it's not always easy being the one who seems to "cause trouble."

If you are labeled as someone who always has a different point of view, you might get a little tired. But one day the pattern will emerge: not bound by one way of thinking, you're the one to discover a solution that isn't obvious or to make a comment that illuminates a thorny problem. (Of course, you may also be tagged the one who is a little loony, a little strange—but it's important to keep in mind that some companies actually RECRUIT people like you and call them corporate "gadflies" or "futurists." And re-member $ecret One: Embrace Your Weirdness!)

The independent thinker is an asset not always appreciated, and it's important to make friends with others like yourself who can appreciate your complexity, so you don't feel so alone. Being all warm, fuzzy, accepted, and cozy with a group is so ORDINARY!

The Outside-the-Box Personality

Are you complex? Do you live mostly outside the box?
Check yourself with the following questions:

1. Y____N____ I have lots of energy, but I also need plenty of quiet and rest.
2. Y____N____ I have both wisdom and childishness, intelligence and openness.
3. Y____N____ I am playful but disciplined.
4. Y____N____ I have a firm grasp of what's real and sensible, but I also have an active imagination.
5. Y____N____ I love to be in the thick of things, but I also need time alone.
6. Y____N____ I am self-assured but I am also shy about my accomplishments.
7. Y____N____ I have both a femme and a macho part of my being.
8. Y____N____ I can be traditional and rebellious.
9. Y____N____ I am passionate about things that inter-est me, but I also know when I've neglected some-thing I find tedious.
10. Y____N____ I experience joy as well as pain.

Ten yes answers, and you definitely live outside the box. More than five yes answers and you're complex enough to tackle most problems in unorthodox ways. Less than five yes answers may mean it's time to turn to the guru of outside-the-box thinking.

Learning How to Think Outside the Box

Mihaly Csikszentmihalyi prescribes three elements for getting outside the box. (In other words if you haven't spent a lifetime outside the box, it's not too late, there are things you can do!)

1. He prescribes "liberating the creative energy of wonder and awe."[1] Unless you see the world as an endlessly mysterious place where there is much to be curious about, your wonder will be stunted.
2. He tells us to practice the habits that support out-of-the-box thinking.
3. He reminds us that once the creative source is freed up, it's of little use unless we apply it.

How to Liberate Wonder and Awe:

⊙ Make schedules to protect your time and avoid distraction; chilling with friends is one thing—being inseparable is another.

⊙ Arrange your physical surroundings to heighten concentration. Do you still have a thousand tchotchkes in your room that are sentimentally important but don't create a serene place for mindfulness? The application of Feng Shui principles can be a big help in creating chi that aids your "out of the box" thinking.

⊙ Cut out meaningless activity so that you have more energy to spend on the things you really care about. If you seem to say YES everytime someone asks for a hand with something, maybe you aren't leaving room for your own brainstorms. Give yourself time to do nothing or devote extra time on a project that just might inspire you.

---

1. Czikszentmihalyi, Mihaly. *Creativity: Flow and the Psychology of Discovery and Invention.* NY: HarperCollins, 1997.

How to Build Habits to Get Out of the Box:

◉ Develop what you lack. Math skills not quite solid? Get a tutor. Never created your own computer program? Tackle that challenge now. Uncomfortable speaking to groups? Get yourself on the program for six or seven organizations and make yourself at home with public presentations.

◉ Shift back and forth from being open to strange and new ideas to being completely focused—blocking out everything to concentrate on something you are trying to achieve. This latter behavior may cause friends to be put off—but if they are REAL friends, they'll respect your need for space, not try to hog it all!

◉ Aim for complexity. What's on the surface is seldom all there is. Make a habit of going deeper, seeking underlying causes, information, news. Lots of people are afraid of complexity because it often puts them out of control. That's okay—out of control is a great place to be sometimes if you want to get out of the box!

How to Use Creative Energy to Solve Problems Out of the Box:

◉ Find a problem. When people around me are bummed out by the magnitude of problems that seem impossible to solve, I'm usually in a great mood—these are the times I know that the most far-fetched ideas will be welcome!

◉ Find a way to express what elements of the problem move you. The best work outside the box occurs not only in the head, but also in the heart. You have to be in touch with what you are feeling, and why, to make it a tool for problem solving.

◉ Look at the problem from as many different points of view as possible. How would your father or mother view this challenge? How would that be different from how your boss might see it? Or the minister in your church? To see something clearly it must be seen from as many perspectives as possible. Sometimes that even means moving physically around a problem. Standing on your head is not a bad way to get a new look at a vexing challenge.

◉ Experiment with many possible solutions. Figure out how each solution might play out differently.

◉ Apply a solution. Out-of-the-box thinking isn't useful if you only *think* about solutions and never try to implement them. If you come up with twenty different menus for a weekend slumber party, but don't do the shopping for any of them, everyone will starve.

Solving World Class Problems, Outside the Box

Here are three world-class challenges aching to be addressed in the first part of the 21st century. What are your solutions? These are sticky problems that a lot of good minds are tackling now. Can you put to work Czikszentmihalyi's prescriptions to get outside the box? Can you offer elegant solutions to complicated problems? Remember that lots of people are spending their entire lives on only one—or part of one—of the questions below. Don't think you have to have an answer in 30 minutes, or even 30 days. You may need 30 years to answer one of these questions.

But give it a shot; take your time. Share the challenges with your friends, and see what kind of solutions you come up with. Notice how you each tackle the problem. There are no rules for how you approach these challenges below. But afterward consider how you came to your solutions. The challenges and their solutions will be posted on **www.dollardiva.com** for you to review and compare. Who knows, maybe your solution will appear there and be recognized by a company that needs your initiative!

Challenge One

The country of Iceland has agreed to put all the DNA records of each of its citizens in a giant data bank for study. What are the benefits and what are the dangers of such a decision? If you were the Queen of Iceland with complete power to decide policy, what would you recommend for this project? Would you ban it? Provide funds so it could roll full steam ahead? Put it in the hands of a few people? Open the data bank online to everyone?

Challenge Two

There are now six billion people on the planet. How many people do you think the earth can support before crashing like a computer with too much information and not enough memory? Can we support twice or three times this number? How? What will life be like? What choices will we make? Should we control population growth? If so, how? If not, what will a planet with 12 billion plus people be like?

Challenge Three

Evil appears to be abundant in the human race. What can we do to decrease acts of violence in our communities? Between countries? In families?

Improve Your Outside-the-Box Skills

What if you look at these three challenges and instead of feeling challenged, you feel clueless? Lost at how to even think about them? You can hone your "outside the box" skills.

⊙ Talk the Talk

Start asking: What if? Why not? How? Adopt the language.

⊙ Take a Vacation

A mental vacation, that is. Experts in creativity know that if you focus on a problem, then walk away and let your mind work on it undistracted, new ideas will come to you when you return to the problem. Sleep is actually a great mental vacation—as is a long shower.

⊙ Learn More About the Problem

Are these three challenges things you never thought about? Get thee to a library! Or journey deep into cyberspace. You can't be creative about something you know nothing about. If the problem interests you, you could spend the next 20 years learning and exploring solutions to any one of these megachallenges!

⊙ Listen to Other People's Solutions

Sometimes an insight comes when, after hearing from others, you begin to detect a pattern in how other people are approaching the problem. Then you can figure out what "outside the box" really means. If the methods of approaching the problem that everyone else has followed don't work, it's time to tackle the problem from a different angle.

⊙ Look for Models

How are other problems solved? Can you apply anything from a problem you have solved previously to the solution of these? Were you the one who figured out how to get more cats spayed in your community? How did you do that, and what lessons did you get from that experience?

⊙ Talk to Experts

Get on the Internet or write letters and track down people who have done work in these fields. See how they approach these problems. If they haven't solved them, then you can still add your "Ah hah!" But it can't hurt to explore the ground that has been covered and see what other people have uncovered so far.

⊙ Model the Problem and Test the Solutions on a Small Scale

Okay, so you can't work directly on the problem. You might be able to create a computer model to work on the solution. Or create a low-tech smaller example of the larger problem, then experiment with small-scale solutions.

⊙ Commit with Passion

Remember Land's advice: Do not undertake the program unless the goal is manifestly important and nearly impossible; do not do anything that anyone else can do readily. The foregoing challenges are the kinds of problems people spend months, years, or lifetimes grappling with. Only take on those challenges so important to you that you can't stop fussing with them!

Gear, Resources, and Actions for Getting Out of the Box

Check Out These Books

Ayan, Jordan E. *Aha!: 10 Ways to Free Your Creative Spirit and Find Your Great Ideas.* New York: Crown Publishing Group, 1997.

MacLean, Barbara Hutmacher. *"I Can't Do What?": Voices of Pathfinding Women.* Ventura: Pathfinder Publishing of California, 1996.

Rosenwasser, Penny. *Visionary Voices: Women on Power: Conversations With Shamans, Activists, Teachers, Artists and Healers.* San Francisco: Aunt Lute Books, 1992.

Try These Organizations
Odyssey of the Mind

609-881-1603

www.odyssey.org

Visit These Web Sites
Empowerment of Girls

www.thefoundry.org/~girlnet

www.next-generation.com/jsmid/news/5509.html

Thinking Visually

www.cbcbooks.org/pubs/gloria.htm

www.whatis.com/outofthe.htm

www.enchantedmind.com

Try This

⊙ Product in a Box™, available through Independent
   Means Inc. 800 350-1816 or **www.dollardiva.com,** is a
   kit designed to guide you through an "out of the box"
   experience by working with materials in a box. Call or
   visit the website to order the kit.

⊙ Create a brainstorming team for your next special event.
   Invite five very different friends and ask them to think
   out loud with you about all the ways you might design
   the event. Put judgments on hold while free heads pre-
   vail! Let the ideas sit for a day or more before making
   choices on next steps.

8 $ecret

Invent

"Invention is the birthing of weird ideas—making them tangible for others to see and use."
—Victoria Groves

Inventors may challenge the laws of physics or break the rules of conventional wisdom. To them the words "You can't do that," are like the red flag to the bull. "You can't" is fuel for the dogged and the determined. Those two words are more likely to make such people prove you wrong than give up.

Inventors are a whole breed of independent thinkers. Independent women are often inventors who channeled their energy in a creative way (Bad grrls may just be inventors who never channeled their energy properly!) and they show up in many different packages:

⊙ **Social inventors** find solutions to complicated social problems. The public library is a social invention that solved the problem of how to give everyone equal access to books and learning. Food rationing is a social invention to deal justly with the agonizing problem of hunger in situations of dire deprivation. Dating is a social invention intended to give couples a means of getting to know one another before mating. (No one has been able to identify the inventor of dating, but historians believe it was a woman in the late Cave Age who was tired of being hauled off by the roots of her hair.)

⊙ **Medical inventors** develop solutions to problems that bedevil human health. The artificial heart, artificial skin, cloning genes, and alternative therapies are all medical inventions that are changing the nature of health care. (Many problems await solutions. For example, we're still waiting for the invention of male pregnancy.)

⊙ **Toy inventors** create new ways to give children and adults delight. A video game or a low-tech board game; a talking doll or a rag doll; a mind-boggling puzzle or a new kind of sculpting material. Toy inventors look for ways to unleash the human capacity for joy and pleasure.

⊙ **Food inventors** look for new foods or new ways to package ancient foods for health. They may make pasta from rice, turn avocados into chips, and make turnips taste like toffee. (The fat-burning chocolate bar could yet make some inventor very wealthy and thin.)

⊙ **Technology inventors** use invention to make things quicker, easier, or safer. They will figure out how to make Star Trek–like ideas real (Beam me up Scottie!), put a woman on Mars, and create cars that run on sunlight or soybean oil. (And the techie who can teleport a screaming child for 30-minute quiet breaks or transform dull speakers into cyberspace entertainers is probably a Nobel Prize contender!)

WHAT KIND OF INVENTOR ARE YOU?

• **SOCIAL INVENTOR?**

• **MEDICAL INVENTOR?**

• **TOY INVENTOR?**

• **FOOD INVENTOR?**

• **TECH INVENTOR?**

Slowing Down a Moonbeam

Usually it takes a moonbeam just over one second to travel to earth. (That's 186,171 miles a second for those of you who are curious.) But a physics team headed by Dr. Lene Vestergaard Hau, Sister Scientist at the Rowland Institute in Cambridge, Massachusetts, recently invented the method for putting the brakes on the speed of light—making it literally possible to slow down a moonbeam and other sources of light for the first time. (Now it's up to you inventors to figure out good applications for slowing down moonbeams!)

Lene Hau is the Danish scientist who leads the project. She expects it will take at least 10 years before major applications are developed (just as some of you are getting out of grad school—good timing!). Why would it be important to slow down the speed of light?

The "Rules" of Invention

1. *Never assume it can't be done just because it hasn't been done.* Most people are wimps and give up on things far too soon.

2. *Never assume you aren't smart enough to solve the problem.* If the problem hasn't been solved it may be because no one has been patient enough to gather all the information required to solve it.

3. *Never assume you have to solve a problem alone to be an inventor.* Knowing how to harness the energy and collective brainpower of a team, or being able to synthesize the discoveries of others, is a key part of the invention process.

4. *Don't beat yourself up when you stumble.* Important discoveries come from failed efforts and great discoveries often build on the earlier mistakes of others. Invention is a collective human endeavor; we're all in this together.

5. *Never miss a chance to ask, "Who said?" or "Why not?"* Inventors question authority. Just because someone else says so isn't a good enough reason to back off—

> **Ancient Inventor**
>
> Shi Dun was an empress and inventor in ancient China. With a member of her staff, the empress developed the first paper from the bark of mulberry trees.

**Women's
History**

Ellen Elgin was
an inventor in
the late 19th
century. She
invented the
clothes wringer
for washing
machines and
in 1888 sold
the patent
rights for $18
because, she
said, "You
know I am
Black and if it
was known that
a Negro woman
patented the
invention,
white ladies
would not buy
the wringer. I
was afraid to
be known be-
cause of my
color."

inventors want to *prove* why something can't be done—
or how it can. (Remember this the next time you are
accused of being too rebellious or independent, perhaps
you should reexamine your potential as an inventor.)

Increase Your "Invention Potential"

Invention potential is aided by doing a few things not typical
among less independent women. Science museums around the
country, documentaries, and even IMAX have reintroduced the
magic of science, invention, and discovery. So if you fall asleep at
the mere mention of biology, go to a cybersite that covers marine
biology and see if you can discover great problems related to the
oceans that need to be solved. The Polar Arctic Ice Cap is melting
at an alarming rate. Do you know what impact that could have on
the world's climate?

Harness Your Passion
The key to invention lies in connecting the things you are passionate about with the things that need to be fixed. Beca Lewis
Allen cares deeply about women acquiring wealth. She invented
The Shift (**www.theshift.com**) to help women get their economic lives together. She wouldn't have invented The Shift if she
didn't care about the problem.

Nothing really gets done unless it's fueled by the energy of
your passion. Does it make you mad that your town doesn't deal
well with the problem of homeless citizens? Great! Use that
anger, that passion, for making a difference and DO SOME-
THING. Look for problems. Where problems can be identified,
inventions can solve them.

Don't Forget to Apply for Patents, Copyrights, Trade-
marks, and Other Legal Claims to Your Creation
It would be so annoying to invent the miniature LineDetector

(sold to women everywhere as they enter bars, concert halls, and other places where rogues and rats congregate) and have someone else collect millions of dollars in licensing fees because you forgot to tell the world the invention was yours.

To figure out how to apply for a patent, go to **www. uspatentinfo.com.** Here you will find a description of the process, registration forms,and a list of organizations that can help you with your patents.

Make Your Invention Pay

Maybe the woman who invented dating didn't have a chance to cash in on her invention. (Though if she had lived in the 20th century she could have claimed her "intellectual property," written about the early days of her discovery, appeared on *Oprah,* and collected royalties from the book sales.) But if you create or invent something, make sure you have the patent. When you invent something valuable, it can create an income for you.

This is the time to write a business plan. It is noble to invent things that make the world a better place. But it's smart to make your nobility pay. Remember you are probably part of the 90 percent of womanhood who WILL have to take care of herself at some point in her life. Why not use your invention to subsidize your retirement or at least that house in Hawaii you want? (See "Gear, Resources, and Actions" for a link to the National Business Plan Competition and an outline for a business plan.)

Do you know any inventors? Do you know which of the following products were invented by women? Test yourself. For each item mark M for man and W for women (answers are at the end of this chapter).

Sad Stats

Between 1841 and 1851, 14 women received U.S. patents. Between 1895 and 1910, 3,615 women received patents. Women still hold less than 2 percent of all patents. Let's GO grrls!

M or W?

_____ The Snugli

_____ The hairbrush

_____ Liquid Paper

_____ Colored signal flares

_____ The permanent wave machine

_____ The digital toaster

_____ The ice-cream freezer

_____ The corset (Now there was a contribution to the world.)

_____ E-Bay.com

Gear, Resources, and Actions for Inventing

Check Out These Books

Haber, Louis. *Black Pioneers of Science and Invention.* New York: Harcourt, Brace, and World, 1970.

Karnes, Ph.D., Frances A. and Suzanne M. Bean, Ph.D. *Girls & Young Women Inventing: Twenty True Stories About Inventors Plus How You Can Be One Yourself.* Minneapolis: Free Spirit Publications, 1997.

MacDonald, Anne L. *Feminine Ingenuity: How Women Inventors Changed America.* New York: Ballantine Books, 1994.

Try These Organizations

Invent America!
P.O. Box 26065
Alexandria, VA 22313
www.ed-pak.com

Women In Technology
www.witi.com

Girl Tech
www.girltech.com
(415) 256-1510

Visit these Web Sites

4000 Years of Women in Science
www.astr.ua.edu/4000WS.html

Invention Dimension
web.mit.edu/invent/www/kids_list.html
www.witi.com

Society of Women Engineers

www.swe.org

www.uspatentinfo.com

See These Videos

October Sky, 1999, starring Laura Dern.

Tucker: The Man and His Dream, 1988, starring Jeff Bridges.

Try This

• If you are between 13 and 19, enter the National Business Plan Competition, **www.dollardiva.com**

These inventions were all created by women!

⊙ The Snugli, by Agnes Auckerman and Ann Moore in 1962.

⊙ The hairbrush, by Lyda Newman in 1898.

⊙ Liquid Paper by Bette Nesmith Graham in 1951.

⊙ Colored Signal Flares by Martha Coston in 1865.

⊙ The digital toaster by Ruane Jeter in 1987.

⊙ The ice-cream freezer by Beulah Henry in 1912.

⊙ The corset by Mary Brush in 1805.

⊙ E-Bay.com by Meg Whitman.

⊙ Donna Dubinsky.

BIG $ecret Three:

Grow Your Money-Self

Quick, answer these questions:

1. Have you ever had a business or been self-employed?
2. Have you ever been a baby-sitter?

Six out of 10 of you probably answered *no* to question 1 and *yes* to question 2. But if you answered 2 with a *yes,* then 1 is also a *yes*! I try this test with every group of women I meet, and it's always the same, regardless of age. Most girls and women forget— or never realized—that baby-sitting is as entrepreneurial a job as mowing lawns or painting houses. *Baby-sitters are entrepreneurs, self-employed business people.*

If you charged for your child-care services you determined the costs of the job (Did you take your own crayons to entertain the kids? Did the parents pick you up or did you have to factor in transportation costs?), what your competitors charge (Do your friends charge $5/hour or $8/hour?), and what the special challenges of the job are (Did you get the twins from hell or is it five kids who require a lot of entertainment?). If you think about how to manage the money you make, you consider how to budget it.

If you work three weekends a month you can purchase that new jacket you saw AND you can set some aside for your college fund.

Grrls who baby-sit are often told they are reliable, great with kids, caring, responsible—and all this is likely true. But they are often not labeled businesslike or entrepreneurial. Meanwhile, the brother who hustles to sell newspapers or mow lawns is considered a budding tycoon, full of initiative, showing real promise, a future entrepreneur, to be sure.

It's this difference in the way women and men are perceived and labeled that affects the female sense of self as an economic being. A distorted, implicit message starts at a very young age that says we can be attractive, helpful, nice, smart, even responsible and reliable, but probably not economically **powerful.**

Well, get over that. If you're going to be independent, you have to be in charge of your own economic life. You have to develop an "income of your own" and manage it so that it grows and works for you and your dreams. Oprah, Madonna, Rosie O'Donnell . . . none of them were born rich, but each now soundly controls her own money and power. And not because they made it as stars, but because they each took charge of the business side of their careers. Fame doesn't make you economically independent. Unless you manage your money as carefully as you manage your love life, your chances for independence dwindle dramatically. The person who signs the checks will always be in charge.

By now you've probably discerned there is a theme in the way $ecrets is spelled in this book: economic power is integral to ALL elements of independence. And this BIG $ecret: Grow Your Money-Self is related to all the other $ecrets.

9 $ecret

Use Your
Money Muscle

"Money for its own sake—or as something you just accumulate and count, is pretty boring. But money as a fertilizer of ideas, possibility, and growth is as exciting as water in the desert. I pay attention to it because it's a great vehicle for giving me choices and the chance to do things that make a difference."
—Jan Seufert

What if Snow White had charged the dwarves $15 an hour for managing their household? She worked the most ridiculous hours. Or what if Cinderella had opened a chain of shoe stores and sold glass slippers that came in a variety of styles and colors, rather than waiting around for some self-important prince to show up with a match for the one she had? Those girls would have told very different stories from the ones we heard.

What's your story going to be? Consider the following scripts:

1. Melissa was an A or B student and went abroad as part of an exchange program. She's had part-time jobs and plans to work for a nonprofit company involved with

environmental advocacy at some point. She still lives at home and spends weekends shopping at the mall.

2. Letoya is incredibly responsible and always juggles a couple of jobs. But she still never seems to have any money—it's all spent, never saved.

3. Janet's life has never been easy. Her parents can't afford to help her out and she works to help with the family's basic living expenses. She has clothes on layaway she can't pay for, and has no idea how she is going to get out of this awful mess.

4. Max has it all. A modest trust fund, an aunt who gives her stock on her birthday, boyfriends who love to buy her things. She studies art and expects to marry someone successful.

Pop Quiz: Who has the most promising economic future? Who's the most independent?

Answer: None of the Above.

That's right, **N.O.T.A**. Whether you are poor or privileged, with a job or without, unless you are in charge of your economic destiny, you are not—cannot be—an independent woman. And the only promise you'll fulfill is to be dependent on someone else for your economic security. Period. The question is, are you waiting for the prince or are you going to market those glass shoes?

> 90 percent of all women (that includes you!) will be solely responsible for their own economic well-being at some point in their life.

Getting Money Savvy

We can curl our hair, apply nail polish, and flirt, all by the tender age of five or six. And we can name the top five music videos at any given time, recall every film Brad Pitt or Harrison Ford ever appeared in, and excel at Six Degrees of Kevin Bacon. Yet managing an income of our own and building prosperity often seems out of reach for too many femmes. We're smart enough to do better. So what **IS** this about?

The answer is complicated and has many parts. But one of the clues to this oddity lies in the way we play as children. It turns out that many (not all) boys develop "informal economies" when they are as young as five or six. That simply means that the kinds of things (vocabulary and skills) you need to know to be economically savvy are simply part of the games they play.

For example, meet my young friends, Shariq and Zaheen Khan, 10 and 12, mentioned earlier in the chapter on taking yourself seriously. One night after dinner, the two brothers were putting their new basketball trading cards in notebooks. I listened as they described each card and talked about how much it was worth. "Here's one worth three hundred dollars," Zaheen said. "I got this thirty-dollar card in a two-dollar pack," the younger Shariq mentioned.

As they talked and reviewed their cards I noticed they were referring to something that looked like a comic book. But it was a newsletter called *Becket's* that listed trading cards—and how much each was worth that month. I'd never heard of *Becket's,* but it seemed a lot like the *Wall Street Journal* of the trading card set to me.

They continued to discuss how much they made buying and selling the cards among their friends at school. "How did you learn to do this?" I finally asked.

They looked at me as though I had two heads. "Do what?" they asked.

"Trade, figure out how much the cards are worth, know what to charge for the cards you sell, what to pay for the cards you buy?"

Shariq, the youngest answered, "I don't know, I've just always known."

Wow. Here was a 10-year-old boy telling me he couldn't remember when he hadn't known how to make a profit. Profit isn't very mysterious. For Shariq and Zaheen, it's just another word for play.

Then I remembered that when they were five or six they were trading pogs. A couple of years after that they traded Magic the Gathering cards. They have an informal economy that is part of their games and social life. Shariq and Zaheen are economically savvy without even trying. When they get a little older and are ready to trade stocks and bonds, it will, in a way, be just the next form of play, no big deal.

"How many girls trade with you at your school?" I asked.

They both thought a minute. "Mmm, maybe one or two," they responded. "Some of them collect the cards, but they don't trade them." In other words, while boys are practicing how to make profits, girls are busy doing other things.

I can argue that the "other things" girls do are every bit as important as the skills Shariq, Zaheen, and their friends acquire through their play. Girls may collect things—and understand long-term value, commitment, and attention. Or maybe girls spend more time developing friendships and taking care of relationships. All this is good work, developed often through play.

But lots of indie wannabes get to the age of 19, 20, and 21 and are clueless about themselves as economic people. By the age of 18 you should:

- ⊙ know how to value your time (when someone says to you, what do I owe you for work you have done, "Whatever you want to pay me" is the wrong answer!),
- ⊙ have a budget,
- ⊙ save money, and
- ⊙ create income.

Maybe you're a whiz at everything on this list and already a tycoon of something. Or maybe you've grown up with a family that made this secret clear to you when you were five. If so, skip on to a different secret to explore. But if you don't know an asset from an astronaut, aren't sure if your liabilities are muscle groups or money concerns, read on.

Five Steps to Money Power

Anyone can:

1. Build a stash.
2. Create a vision.
3. Establish what you are worth.
4. Learn the language of money.
5. Create income.

Here's how:

Build a Stash

It's not enough to make money. Unless you set some aside regularly, the money you make will do nothing but get you by. Independence requires money you can use to:

a. make dreams come true
b. get you out of a jam
c. give you freedom to make choices
d. keep you safe
e. make a difference

A stash is money that is set aside *and* growing. It's not just those coins you save in jars under the bed. It's money that grows from interest earned and assets that become more valuable as time goes by. Whether it's 10 percent of every night's income from baby-sitting or 10 percent of your monthly salary from your job as a TV producer, the proceeds from turning in those long read (and now forgotten) books to the local used bookstore, or that annual birthday gift from Uncle Jack, you have to build a stash that grows.

If you have the discipline to lose five pounds or the willpower to get up before dawn and swim laps three times a week, or if you have the imagination to write a poem or pen song lyrics, you have what it takes to create a stash. Start with small goals. Can you save $25 in three months? (You probably spend that much on CDs in a month. Make a sacrifice, listen to someone else's CD—let them throw their money away.)

If you can save $25 in three months, you can save $100 in a year. If you can save $100, you can invest in stock. See the chart below to see how money grows once you have a stash! You can do this. (How much did you spend on shoes last year? French fries? Lipstick?)

Look at what happens to money saved in a regular way:

You Save: (at 7% Annual compounded interest)	2 Yrs. Later:	5 Yrs. Later:	10 Yrs. Later:
$10/month (1 tube of lipstick or 3 Big Macs)	$256.81	$715.93	$1,730.85
$20/month (2 movies or 3 bottles of nail polish)	$513.62	$1,431.00	$3,461.00

So what's it going to be? Some color to put on your nails? Onion rings that travel to your hips and coat your heart in fat? Rent the video, buy your Levi's at a secondhand shop, and make your own coffee. If you can save $1,431 just by doing without a couple of bottles of nail polish a month, you could have a start toward a down payment on a car. (Did someone say independence?)

But let's say you have the tenacity of a marathon runner. You leave the money alone and let it continue to build—that $20/month will grow to over $10,000 in 20 years! (Let's call that start-up capital, or the down payment on a house—get the picture?) Of course as you grow older, you'll make more money and put more away. Take a look at what happens if you start saving seriously by the age of 25:

You Save: (at 7% compounded interest)	You're 40— it becomes:	At 50 (You're ready to take a loooong vacation!):
$200/month Have a job as a forest ranger, earn $2500/month	$63,392.46	$162,014.34
$350/month You're a translator at the U.N., make $4000/month.	$110,936.80	$283,525.09
$500/month Freelance computer programmer, average $10,000/month.	$158,481.15	$405,035.85

See how after a while, with a large enough stash, money starts to make money while you sleep? You can do this. If you have to start with $1 a week it's okay. Start. Get in the habit. If you're serious about independence, this is a must.

Create a Vision

Setting aside money for the sake of accumulating money is pretty boring. Money is the vehicle that allows you to put your dreams in place. But a vision is a plan on paper that makes the dreams you have in your head tangible and attainable.

Do you want to visit Paris? Take salsa lessons? Buy a car? Maybe you want to make a contribution to the family budget or, conversely, are planning an escape from home to an apartment of your own. Perhaps you have a plan to experiment with low-cost shelter for the homeless. Do you see yourself traveling the world for a year after college before starting your job? Maybe you'd like to start an internet zine or collect silver thimbles. Whatever you have in mind for yourself, it probably has a cost. So get your vision on paper and create a plan.

Try this. Draw a circle. Inside that circle, write or draw the most important idea you have for yourself for the next year. Now make other circles that represent other goals, interests you'd like to pursue. This is what my personal map looks like right now. (Though it changes a little every few years, as some goals are attained and others come into view.)

Life Map Vision

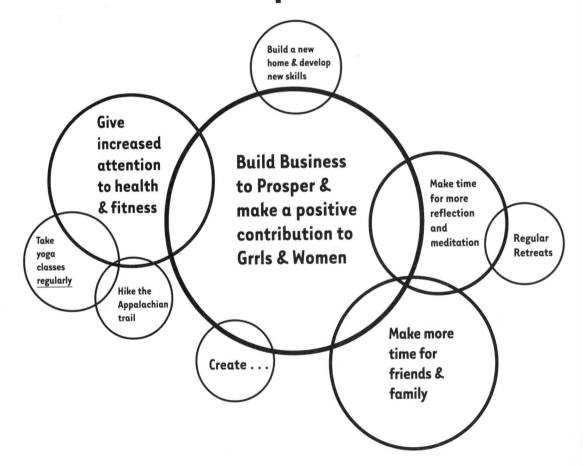

A map of your vision is personal, everyone's will look different. But once you have it you can create a "vision plan." Do the same thing again, but this time think about how you want that map to look five years from now. Do it again five years after that. And five years after that . . .

Establish What You Are Worth

There are at least three ways to think about what you're worth. And you need to keep them *all* in mind.

Your inner worth

This is the beauty invisible to the eye that is luminous with your life force. Your inner worth has no price tag. You're in charge of this. Indie women seem to possess the knowledge of their worth. They take themselves seriously and that forces others to take them seriously, too.

Grrl with a Vision

Katy Meyer was 14 when she decided to turn her passion for painting into her stash source. She had taken an art class and learned to paint on silk. That same year she created a business plan for selling silk scarves. She had to source the silk, practice different designs to see what would sell, and develop her technique to make sure she had some consistency in her scarves (otherwise she would lose a lot of money on silk she had to throw away).

Slowly her business grew. By the time she was a freshman in college she was taking special orders for wall hangings that she could sell for $800. Her regular scarves sold for $40 to $180 apiece. She never went anywhere without a few scarves and as soon as she displayed them, they sold out.

Her scarf business was not a cute hobby or just a casual pastime. It was a venture she took seriously and forced others around her to take seriously. By the time she was ready to think about college, she knew she wanted a school that would allow her to continue to pursue her two paths of art and business. Colleges, eager to please someone with such a clear vision, were thrilled to help build a program around her needs.

Katy's mom and dad divorced when she was 13. She couldn't count on easy cash from her parents, so she created an income of her own. Not everyone will create a business when they're 14. Some teenage women decide to get experience and earn money by taking a part-time job working for someone else. Whatever the income source, it's important to see it not as something you do as a kid to earn spending money, but as part of your life plan to take care of yourself.

How highly do you regard yourself? What is your inner sense of your value? Everyone has value by virtue of being human and taking up space on earth. Still, it's easy to feel worthless some days, and if you make a habit of it, you will have a hard time getting up in the morning. Nurturing your inner being, respecting your own value, is critical. At 21 or 30 (or 40 or 50 or 60) it's easy to get sidetracked by O.P.O. (other people's opinions), but the really independent woman remembers that her inner worth is something she determines herself.

Your Net Worth

Your net worth is actually easier to keep track of than your inner worth. Do the following. Take out a notebook (or do this on your computer and keep a record of it), and enter the appropriate information. Here's a sample of Spenderella Sampson's accounts; (You'll meet her in the chapter on investing.)

Everything I own:	
Savings bonds	$1000 (a gift from my grandmother)
Savings account	$25
The pearl necklace my mother gave me	$250
Car (it's used, old, but it runs, and it's paid for)	$850
Computer (it really belongs to my dad, so I can't add it)	$0
Stocks or real estate (this is before I met Irene)	$0
A copyright I put on that poem published a few years ago.	$50
Other:	
	TOTAL: $2175
Everything I owe:	
The $50 still due for that jacket on layaway	$50
Car payments	$0
School loans	$0
The money borrowed from my mother last month	$125
The $15 I borrowed from (Sam) when we were at the mall last week.	$15
Credit card debt	$450
	TOTAL: $640

Fill in your chart:

Everything I own:	
Savings	
Possessions	
Stocks or real estate	
Other	
Other	
Other	
	TOTAL:
Everything I owe:	
Credit cards	
Car payments	
School loans	
Money borrowed from friends/family	
Other	
Other	
	TOTAL:

Net Worth=
What I own
minus what I
owe.

Okay, now subtract everything you owe from everything you own. That number is your current net worth. Is it positive? Do you own more than you owe? Great start. Or is it negative, do you owe more than you own? If it's the latter it's not worth a panic, but it is time *to deal!!!!*

And the only way to deal is to take charge of building your net worth. This has nothing to do with age—remember Shariq and Zaheen? Not only are they able to trade and make money, they are probably able to figure out their net worth in a New York minute and they haven't even hit their teen years yet! So fill in the following. *Income sources* (Now):

    Likely or possible gifts: _____

    Sale of something I own (used textbooks, dresses I no longer
        wear): _____

    Job income: _____

Subsidy (what someone else pays for now that eventually I will be responsible for): _____

Expenses:

Loans (from college): _____

Entertainment (movies, music, etc.): _____

Self-care (makeup, clothes, etc.): _____

Living (food, shelter, transportation): _____

Other:_____

Money set aside for your stash: Take 10 percent of your income number and make that your monthly sum to set aside.

Is your income greater than your expenses? Can you set aside 10 percent or more for a stash? **If not, you have three options:**

1.   Cut expenses (rent a video, make your own popcorn).
2.   Increase income.
3.   Better yet, do both.

The Worth of Your Salable Skills

If you decide to wash cars in the neighborhood next week so that you can buy a birthday present for your best friend, how do you figure out what to charge? How did Katy Meyer know what to charge for her scarves? How do you figure out what to ask for when you find out that the promotion you wanted has come up? The answer to all these situations is the same.

Figure out the fixed costs *of the job.* If you buy wax to polish the cars you wash, add that to the cost of the sponge you bought (unless you borrowed it from your mom's garage). When Katy Meyer was figuring out what to charge for her scarves, she had to know what the silk cost (including how much it cost to get it shipped to her house), as well as the cost of the paint she used and the cost of building the frame she worked on. Add the costs of the job together.

Figure out what you will charge for your time. But remember, at every age, women almost always undercharge for their time—it's tied to a sense of inner worth. Don't get trapped in that pit!! If you were to take a similar job working for someone else, what's the going rate for that job? Same thing if you are promoted from assistant director to director. What are other people with the same job title making at that level?

And watch those job titles, too! A national news anchor tells of one of her first jobs in television. She was given an assignment as the Coordinator for Women and Minorities. "What are the men in this job called?" she asked. "Producers," she was told. They were paid $20/hour more than she. Do not undersell yourself. And don't let others underpay you with their sly tricks!

Figure in a margin. When Katy was pricing her scarves, she figured her costs (the silk, the paint, her time, et cetera) and then she determined her margin. If her costs were $20 and she decided to sell the scarf for $40, she had a 100 percent margin.

Katy had to charge more than it cost to make the scarf. And then, because her scarves were special, the market would pay an additional sum. Why do you pay $60 for a pair of Calvin Klein jeans when you can pay $30 for the brand from Sears? Because you like the way they look, you want his label to show over your right hip, in other words, you, as the market, will pay whatever extra he can charge. If Katy suddenly faces a lot of competition from designers who make scarves like hers, and her customers want a hand-painted scarf for $25 rather than $40, she will have to adjust her margin to stay in business, or maybe she will buy cheaper silk and cut her costs.

Figuring out what to charge is like working a puzzle. It can be fun—but you do have to pay attention to the details!

Figure out your price. Add the costs of the job to the costs of your time, and calculate your margin, and there you have whatever you are going to charge for your skills or your product. And remember, whatever that price is, the customer must really want it and be willing to pay it, or it won't sell.

One caution: don't allow someone else to set the value of your time or product. I often ask women what they charge for their services and all too often they will answer that they take whatever the person who has hired them thinks they should get. BAD PRACTICE!! If you're going to be in charge of your economic destiny, you'll figure out what you're worth and not be embarrassed to ask for it.

Learn the Language

Which language did you study to fulfill your school's language requirement? French? Spanish? Mandarin? Business? Business, how did that sneak in? Business is, to some extent, just another language to master.

You understand that if you want a really memorable trip to Mexico, it's better to understand the culture and speak the language. Business is the same: You have to understand the culture and speak the language. If you are going to master your economic destiny you have to master the language to get there.

What is profit? Net income? A copyright? An asset? A debit? What's a consignment? A commission? Think you don't know those words? Well, if you have ever taken a dress you no longer wear to a secondhand shop to resell, you probably did it on *consignment*. When your dress was resold, you received a percent of the *profit*. And remember that short story you wrote that the local newspaper asked permission to print last month? If you didn't retain the *copyright,* you gave up an *asset*. Business language is not for use someday in the distant future—it is part of your present so-called life, right now.

Learning business language is not like trying to master brain surgery. Here are seven ways to begin:

- Read the business section of the newspaper. Okay, some business writers are incredibly boring. Hang in there, doing laps some mornings can be pretty monotonous too, but you do it with a larger purpose in mind—you know this is good for your body, your speed, your discipline!!

- For stories that ARE fun, get your hands on magazines like *Inc., Fast Company,* or *Working Woman.* You can read

them on-line; their on-line addresses are at the end of
the chapter.

I once interviewed an exchange student from Japan
who was doing an internship at a company in Minneapolis. She seemed more sophisticated than most 19-year-
olds I had met, sure of herself, full of plans and dreams.
"How did you get such a clear sense of direction?" I
asked her over lunch.

"I used to steal my father's *Business Week* magazine
every week and read it in my bedroom," she answered.

I don't know where that young woman is now, but I'm
willing to bet she is back in Japan, building a career that
makes her happy!

◉ If you don't know what words mean, ask around until
you find someone willing to help you understand. The
only dumb question is the one not asked. (A mentor can
also be a good aid for building your business language.

◉ Take a business course.

◉ Intern in a woman-owned company—and listen.

◉ Rent *Empire Records, Boiler Room, Woman of the Year, Nine to
Five, Baby Boom,* and *Norma Rae.* See if you can figure out
the business issues in those movies. (Remember they are
movies, not necessarily accurate reflections of real life!)

OK, you know you need a stash. You have a vision (or you're
working on it). You know your worth (or you will soon), and
you're building a business vocabulary. There's just one catch: you
need a source of income. Now what?

It's Time to Create an Income of Your Own!
Check all of the following that apply to you.

1. __ I have a part-time job.
2. __ I have a generous father/mother who gives me
whatever I need.

3. ___ I am starting/have a business of my own.
4. ___ I own stocks or have invested in mutual funds.
5. ___ I have a copyright on something I have written.
6. ___ I have received a patent for one of my inventions.
7. ___ I own land that was left to me by a relative.
8. ___ I get an allowance.
9. ___ I have money in a savings account.
10. ___ A great aunt left me an oil well in Texas.
11. ___ Other (please describe).

If you checked any of the above, you have a start toward creating income. But you still have a long way to go. You have a job? Great. What happens when you're laid off because your job is no longer necessary? You have a generous father? What happens when you're 21 and he says, "okay, kid, you're on your own." Or worse, what if your mom or your dad gets laid off and you're on your own at 18? Not unusual. You have money in a savings account? Fine, what's it doing?

The point is, one source of income isn't enough. Remember that saying your grandmother used to mutter? *Don't put all your eggs in one basket.* The trick to building a lifelong income (big enough to support your dreams) is to create more than one source of income and manage that income with a plan. And if you didn't mark ANY sources of income, then get a move on!

Whether you're 16 or 26, consider the following ideas as inspiration for ways of creating income for yourself:

- ◉ *Turn things you no longer use into income.* Do you have a killer Barbie collection? Put an ad in the local paper; a serious Barbie collector may pay top dollar for it. Does that bright orange coat you loved last year now make you nauseated? Take it to the local secondhand store and see if you can sell it on consignment. (Someone may love it!)

- ◉ *Try the unconventional.* Your town never had grrls on the

UGH!

About 40 percent of women over 65 are poor, compared to just 13 percent of men who are poor over the age of 65.

UGH!

◉ Caucasian Women earn only $0.75 for every dollar a man earns.
◉ African-American women earn only $0.63.
◉ Hispanic women earn only $0.56.
Make a job, don't just take a job, is the way to fix this problem!

construction crew? Now is the time to make change and earn some money you can actually count.

◉ *Create a partnership with a friend or relative.* Together, grow fresh vegetables to sell at a farmer's market next summer or make and deliver specially decorated jack-o'-lanterns for Halloween. Maybe she supplies the cash for seeds and you do the labor. Or you decorate the jack-o'-lanterns and create the marketing brochure and she makes the deliveries.

◉ *Sell something you now make for fun.* Do you make the best lemon squares in the neighborhood? Maybe you can work out a deal with a local bakery to supply them with a couple of dozen they can sell. Or do you have the coolest nails in town because you have mastered the art? Sell your services to friends. (Ten manicures gets you a free pedicure? Sign me up!)

◉ *Work for free and invent a project that will pay you money.* Do you think you want to be an architect but have no skills and can't imagine why anyone would hire you? Offer to do a six-week internship in a firm that will let you do odd jobs for nothing. If you're smart and observant, by the end of that time, you will have found something that needs to be done and can offer to do the project for a fee. If you do the job well, you may land yourself a paying summer job. But you have to take the risk, and you have to work hard.

◉ *Start submitting those short stories you write to magazines that might pay you for your work.* Don't forget to register the copyright!

◉ *Make a deal with family members for shares of stock.* Substitute stock in place of a more traditional birthday gift. I know this seems like a tough choice but go back and review your net worth and think it over!

◉ *Get a job.* I know you have a busy social life and maybe your boyfriend will complain. Remember Snow White?

She spent a lot of time on those dwarves. Had she been earning money while she lived with them, she could have bought a bus ticket out of the forest without waiting for some prince who probably had bad breath.

You get the idea, there are many ways to make money. And if you want **maximum freedom,** you'll use your crazy/weird/original/wonderful ideas to start building your stash.

A Public Service Announcement from the Author

Having a lot of money does not guarantee either happiness or security. I don't measure my success by the size of my paycheck. I never have, though many people do. I've driven the same car for 10 years, and my close friends know I care more about following my heart than doing things I hate to make someone else happy because he or she controls my paycheck.

Truly independent people don't get themselves locked into lifestyles they can't support. Still, in my head is a picture of a perfect house, built like a great treehouse. I want to realize that dream. And I like being able to write a check to support the causes I feel strongly about. But making a lot of money just to buy a faster car, more clothes, or to impress so-called friends has never made much sense to me.

The point of understanding your worth, creating a stash, and building economic power is to make choices and control your destiny, whatever your dreams may be. Two of my favorite books are *Living the Good Life* by Scott and Helen Nearing and *Small Is Beautiful* by E. F. Schumacher. Both offer a vision of life that is exciting, spiritual, and fulfilling. But the authors all understood—and did in their own lives—the exercises in this chapter!

Gear, Resources, and Actions for Using Your Money Muscle

Check Out These Books

Harroch, Richard D., Jerome S. Engel. *Small Business Kit for Dummies.* Indianapolis: IDG Books Worldwide, 1998.

Godfrey, Joline. *Our Wildest Dreams.* New York: Harper Collins Business, 1989.

Sander, Jennifer Basye. *101 Best Extra-Income Opportunities for Women.* Garden City: Doubleday Direct, 1997.

Visit these Web Sites

www.nawbo.org

www.few.org

www.dollardiva.com

www.futurescan.com

www.ideacafe.com

www.onlinewbc.org, SBA's Online Women's Business Center

Try These Organizations

American Business Women's Association

National Association of Women Business Owners

See These Videos

The Baby Sitters Club, 1995.

Baby Boom, 1987.

Read These Magazines

Working Woman, **www.workingwomanmag.com**

Fast Company, **www.fastcompany.com**

Young Money

Inc.

Try This

Create a Personal "Annual Report."

- ⊙ Write an introduction reviewing the social and financial actions of the last year, and stating your goals—social and financial for the coming year.
- ⊙ List all your assets and debts.
- ⊙ Describe actions to be taken to reach the goals stated.
- ⊙ Circulate your "Report" to close friends and family for feedback—and accountability.

$ecret 10.

Invest

"I don't gamble. I make intelligent choices about what matters and what I want to make an investment in."
—Brooke Espinoza

Make money while you sleep. Sound appealing? This is not a pipe dream if you start investing this month.

Remember Shariq and Zaheen and the trading card story? Too many grrls hear "stocks, investment, and equity" and feel some inner fire alarm—as in "Ohmigod I need to DO something but I have no idea what."

Deciding it would take a different strategy to encourage some of you to explore investing, I chose to demystify this secret by embedding it in the form of a story. The two main characters, Irene and her slightly ditzy, but consumer-sly friend Sara, are certified DollarDivas.

Learning How to Invest

**High
Anxiety**

70 percent of
women worry
they will not
have enough
money when
they are older.

The story that unfolds here is set in Santa Monica, California. It's late afternoon on a warm April day . . .

Sara was having a mocha at Starbucks® when her classmate, Irene (aka the Investment Queen, behind her back), walked in. Irene ordered a tall skinny latte with vanilla and was waiting for her coffee when Sara called out, "Hey girl, where have you been keeping yourself? I haven't seen you in two moons!"

Sara looked fine sitting in the corner in her long sleeved emerald green dress, gaily patterned Birkenstocks gracing her feet, and three bead bracelets on her wrist. Irene couldn't help frowning as she walked over to Sara's table. "I see you've been putting money on your back again," she remarked sarcastically.

Sara and Irene had just finished their junior year of college. They had known each other since junior high and had had an ambivalent relationship over the years. Irene was sensible and careful; Sara was seemingly without a care to weigh her down. In fact, the two opposites had a grudging respect for one another, but they had never been able to call a truce long enough to get to know each other.

Slow Start:

The average
age of first in-
vestment for
women is 47
years old.
*At least 27
years too late.*

"Chill out, girl," Sara advised her. "Sit down, drink your latte and tell me about your plans for the summer." Sara was feeling generous. She had just learned that the summer job she wanted at a hat boutique on 3rd Street had come through. Her starting pay was twelve dollars/hour with an enviable 30 percent discount on all goods. What she could do with that in the outlet! She couldn't wait.

"Well," Irene started, "I'm taking a course in investment trends at Santa Monica City College and I have an internship at the Pacific Stock Exchange downtown."

"An internship! That doesn't pay anything does it?" Sara asked.

"Well no, but it's part of a bigger plan I have to get more experience in investment and finance," said Irene.

Sara almost sneered, "You are so boring, Irene. You won't be going to any concerts this summer and, as usual, won't have any money to party—what do you think you'll get out of your internship other than an A in Advanced Econ next year?"

Irene felt her temper rise and her face turn red. "While I'm wasting my life in all these boring pursuits as you call them, it looks like you're wasting your time and money on clothes, more clothes, stupid jewelry, and anything else that will keep you looking good but will have no impact on the rest of your life—you may think I'm boring, but you're just plain short-sighted. I've already saved enough to visit my grandparents in Hawaii before school starts."

Having finished her heated defense of herself, Irene slammed her latte on the table and stalked out. She was angry—but she was also hurt and feeling foolish. Why, she wondered, didn't Sara and her crowd understand that she HAD to think ahead? Why did they make fun of her for being a little different from them? She'd like to be like Sara every now and then—but she didn't know how. All she knew was that life was hard, her mother struggled to make ends meet, and if she wanted to finish college, she had to keep her priorities straight.

Meanwhile, Sara was feeling a little foolish, herself. She wished she could learn something from Irene and just didn't know how to ask. She suspected that independent Irene really knew a lot about how to make money grow and that, down the road, she would have a lot more freedom than Sara. Why couldn't they build a relationship? Sara would be happy to show Irene how to loosen up and Lord knew Sara would like to know more about how to make money while she slept! Slightly less burdened by pride than Irene, Sara was determined to work something out with her touchy friend. That night she e-mailed the following message to her soon to be investment guru:

Irene—it's nuts for us to torment one another when we could team up instead. How about a truce: you teach me how to invest this summer and I'll have you looking fine for that internship you're so keen on.
—Sara

Irene wasn't stupid. She saw that she could invest in herself in a new way and make peace with Sara. She e-mailed back:

You're on. Here's how we begin . . .
—Irene

And that was the start of the Summer Adventure of Irene the Investment Queen and Sara "Spenderella" Sampson. By the time they graduated from college the next year, Irene was dressed for success and Sara was investing for success. The two did not have an easy time learning from one another—there would always be an edge in their relationship—but each could see the other had something to teach and in the end they were both learners, more hungry for new information than determined to self-destruct by behaving stupidly.

Sara did not get rich that first summer. Irene wouldn't even let her spend any money on stocks—she made her *save* money while she was learning what a stock was. And Irene finally developed a style of her own. Though she wasn't chosen for a photo shoot as a *Jane* model, she was featured in *Fast Company* magazine as the smartest intern hired by the Pacific Stock Exchange.

But by the time she graduated from college, Sara had a cool $5,000 in savings, investments in her portfolio, and a plan for growing her money. She was pretty proud of herself and though she found it hard to tell Irene, grateful to see how she could now fund some of her more offbeat dreams—like opening a school for windsurfers and building a house in Bali.

7 Steps to Investing

Here are the 7 steps Irene shared with Sara that summer and through their senior year in college. If Sara could do this, you can too.

1. Start Saving

First she needed money to invest with—all that cash she'd been putting on her back had to be channeled to a new purpose: savings. When they figured out how much Sara paid for clothes, earrings, and lipstick every month, it came to a whopping 30 percent of all the money she received from her part-time job, the birthday gifts from her aunts and grandmothers, and the clothes she "recycled" every month on consignment at the local thrift store.

Irene made her scale back and promise to spend only 5 percent on anything she could wear and put the other 25 percent into a Certificate of Deposit account until they were ready to invest. For Irene, on the other hand, to go from spending nothing on how she looked to spending five percent of what she made in her job after school was a big deal—she finally got a haircut that made her look exotic instead of simply unkempt. And a college intern at the Exchange started to pay serious attention . . . but that's another story. . . .

2. Identify Products

While Sara was rearranging the way she spent money and putting aside some to invest (it would be three months before she actually bought stock), Irene had her list products she liked, used, and knew something about. Here are a couple of e-mails they exchanged during this time:

> You asked what products or companies I trust. Well, I wear Gap™ clothes, and everyone I know shops at the Gap. So I guess that's one I'd

The Investor Chick's Lingo

Bulls believe stock market prices will rise. Bears think the prices will go down. Sooner or later both are going to be right. The trick is investing for the long term and not getting distracted or anxious about bears and bulls!

have to include. My parents bought me an iMac® for my birthday and though I know you work on a PC now, I love my Mac and wouldn't change for anything, so that's my second choice. And though I really love Bobbi Brown™ cosmetics, I've switched to Australis™ because they are way more affordable. I can tell you that Windjam makes the best windsurfing boards on the market. I've been spending a lot of time at Home Depot™ lately (my mom has a bug for renovation and they have some very cool classes). And when I was watching CNNfn last night (this is not MTV for sure), someone mentioned an aquaculture company that sounded cool—what is aquaculture anyway?

—Sara

3. Research the Products/Companies.

Good start Sara, now go find out everything you can about these products and companies—if any of them still look good after doing a Nancy Drew on them, we'll put them in your 'maybe buy' list. Check the Web, ask around, get to the library and get back to me.

—Irene

Ten days later, Sara not only knew what aquaculture was, she knew the stock price of all the products she had listed, had the inside skinny on the challenges and possibilities of each company, and was having a great time gathering the 411 on companies the way she used to on her friends. This was infinitely more interesting! She reported back to Irene.

Gap's latest campaign was a hit (did you love those ads?) and their stock is trading in the midthirties; Apple's latest line of computers is even more powerful than anyone had predicted and the loyal core of Mac fanatics know this company is fly again! And did you know that Bobbi Brown is owned by Estee Lauder? Who knew? Lauder seems to be buying up everyone—except Australis—wish I could get hold of THAT stock!

And that aquaculture company I mentioned went belly up last

SOME PLACES TO INVEST $$

- **MUTUAL FUNDS**
- **INDEX FUNDS**
- **TREASURY BILLS, NOTES, OR BONDS.**
- **INDIVIDUAL STOCKS**
- **REAL ESTATE**
- **YOURSELF**

month, but there are a couple of other aquaculture companies I found that are growing and expanding to meet demand from people in Japan who are importing fish for their own use. I can't buy any Windjam stock. It's privately owned by some chick in Baja, and she's not sure she wants to sell any equity right now—but the boards are certainly selling. What a life she leads! Selling windsurfing boards and living on the beach while cashing checks that come in from the stores selling her boards around the world! So what do you think? And Home Depot is still growing like weeds in the back alley—that looks like a great company for a long time to come. Is it time to buy?

—Sara

4. Monitor the Stocks

Slow down, Sara. Just keep an eye on the stocks you like for a while and see what they do—if your instincts still look good in a month, we'll make an investment. Meantime, read, stay on top of these companies, and keep building that nest egg!

—Irene

By September, Sara had saved a remarkable $1,000. (She netted $300 a week from her job at the boutique and really did save 25 percent of her summer income just as Irene had dictated.) She hated passing up that little black Donna Karan dress she'd seen on sale in July, but she had a bigger vision in her head these days than a few yards of cloth. Finally, Irene agreed that it was time to buy stock.

Sara was clueless about what this meant or how to do it. Where did you go? Who did you talk to? Irene said they could buy stock on the Web and she had visited a lot of sites that wanted her money—but which ones could she trust? How much did it cost? What should she do? She e-mailed Irene again:

5. Research How to Make an Investment

> Okay, Irene, I've got the money, we've decided which stocks I should
> buy—but how do I buy them?
> —Sara

> How did you figure out where to buy those windsurfing boards you al-
> ways talk about? How did you track down that underground video game
> you wanted?
> —Irene

> I asked around, talked to people, I did what I do best—check things out.
> —Sara

> Do the same here. E-mail those Web sites you've been visiting and see
> what they say. Then call a couple of companies and see who will talk
> with you and who's helpful and who's not. Some companies have a min-
> imum investment amount that you can't cover yet. And, I can tell you
> that investing for the long term, you'll want to consider mutual funds
> and index funds as well. Let me know what you find out.
> —Irene

Irene didn't make anything easy for Sara. But Irene knew that
whatever Sara learned on her own she would understand better
than anything she could tell her. And she did recognize that Sara,
if more of a free spirit than herself, was no dummy. She had
learned to trust her new protégée's ability to learn.

A few days later, Sara e-mailed Irene again.

> I found out that I can't legally invest on my own until I'm 18—so on
> my next birthday I'll be ready. But in the meantime, my Aunt Jane
> agreed to open a "custodial" account for me through her brokerage
> firm. I've written a check for $1000 to her and we talked for a while
> about what I want to buy. She suggested something she called index
> funds and mutual funds—which I'm going to start learning about. But I

told her I wanted to start with a stock I know and can watch daily. What do you think?

—Sara

It's like everything else, if it works for you, go with it. Have your aunt purchase the stocks for you and see how things go for the next few months. By your birthday, you can open an account of your own and will also have a better idea of what mutual funds and index funds are as well. And by then you'll also have enough money to meet the investment levels of companies like Charles Schwab.

—Irene

6. Invest and Monitor the Service You Receive

Sara made her purchases through her aunt and Irene didn't hear from her for a few weeks. She figured Sara felt she could continue learning on her own and didn't need Irene any longer. Then the stock market dropped by over 300 points and Sara called Irene in a panic. "Okay, girl, I worked hard for that money and now they are way below what I paid for them. What's your advice now, Ms. Investment Queen?"

7. Choose Between Long-term and Short-term Investments

Irene calmly asked Sara: "Are the companies in that fund still good companies or did something happen to make them less trustworthy in the last couple of weeks?"

"As far as I can see, they're on track—but that doesn't matter, the market went so far down today I'm afraid it will never go back up."

"It does matter," Irene argued. "We agreed you were investing in solid companies that have good long-term prospects. The only risk you decided to take was with that aquaculture company you wanted to invest in. If you have a cow every time the stock market goes up and down you'll be a nervous wreck and drive me crazy. Watch the companies, make sure you are in this for the long term, and don't panic."

Three weeks later, Irene received another call from Sara. "You were right, Irene. The market has calmed down and my stocks have regained their value. Even that aquaculture company looks like it may be ready to take off—I read the other day that the Asian market for fish is picking up again. Even so, I think I'll start to invest in funds I don't have to watch so carefully and leave individual stocks until I have more time to pay attention. The return potential may be bigger on some of those sexy individual Internet stocks, but I have to focus on my studies now if I have any hope of switching into that marine biology major course I want. Any ideas?"

Of course Irene had ideas, and she and Sara began a new course on longer-term investments like mutual funds, that would grow while Sara focused on her future as a marine biologist who could set up a lab in Bali and windsurf on her days off!

Rules for Investing

The rules for investing that Irene shared with Sara were not exotic formulas for rocket science. Basically, Irene coached Sara to:

1. Pay Attention to What You Know
You know what you like and find useful. And you know what your friends are using. If a company uses sweatshops to make its products, you've probably heard and don't buy there—that's not a great long-term investment. If the product is the sort of thing everyone knows will be here today, gone tomorrow, that's probably not where you want to put money either. The point is, you know more than you think you do. Sara watched the stocks of companies that she liked, used, and knew something about. When she was ready to invest, she felt as though she invested in something less alien than it had earlier seemed.

2. Invest for Long-term Growth. Ignore "Hot Tips."

This is not the race track! Don't get dazzled by stocks just because they are in the news and popular. Try to identify companies that build for value and have long-term visions and steady (sometimes less flashy) growth.

3. Learn About Companies, Mutual Funds, and Index Funds.

Buying stock is like buying anything else. If you don't do your homework, you deserve to get bitten. And as Sara learned, doing research on your investments can actually be a lot of fun (and has a better pay-off than following the usual gossip about the girl who moved to town from someplace in Europe). And like anything else, the more information you gather, the better off you are. It's probably not enough just to surf the Web for information—though that's important. It's also essential to talk to people who know something about the companies and the funds you are exploring, and read back issues of magazines and newspapers that report on them. (Any skeletons in the company closet?) Study their annual reports, and don't forget to trust your intuition.

4. Watch What They Do for a While.

Like that incredibly attractive character who lives in your apartment building, not everything is as good as it looks. It doesn't hurt to take your time watching what happens with a stock or a fund. Once you have some practice reading the stock pages, figuring out how to tell a pretty stock from one that is really substantive, you'll have confidence in your own judgment.

5. Buy.

There are a lot of ways to invest. You can have a broker do it for you. (They charge you a fee every time you buy or sell something.) You can buy through the Web. (There's still a fee, but it tends to be lower.) You can join an investment club and buy as part of a group. Or, if you are under 18 and not of legal age to invest on your own, ask someone in your family to set up a "custodial account" for you.

6. Build a Portfolio.

A financial portfolio (like a portfolio of manuscript samples or artwork) is a collection of different stocks and equity interests. Just a year after she started, Sara's portfolio included a Schwab index fund, the shares of Apple and Gap stock she owned, as well as the shares of H_2OFish, the aquaculture stock she bought. As she grew savvier and more familiar with her comfort zone of risk, she decided to keep about five percent of her portfolio in riskier start-up company stocks, about 60 percent in mutual funds, 25 percent in an international fund, and 10 percent in cash equivalents.

But everyone's formula is a little different. For a good guide to figuring out YOUR formula, you might check out *Charles Schwab's Guide to Financial Independence* (see the Gear section for how to get it). Clear and easy to follow—it would have been a great help to Sara had Irene not been around!

Every independent grrl has a financial portfolio—and every independent woman has her own unique collection in her portfolio.

7. Manage It and See How You Do.

The most dangerous words you can utter: "I'll let someone else do it for me." No one cares about your portfolio as much as you will—it's your money, your future, your own interests. Too many people, including celebrities who should have known better, have horror stories to tell for allowing "someone else" to do it. In the end, managing your money, in all its forms, is something only you can do.

8. Don't Impulse Buy.

The buzz around town is that a new vitamin is on the market that melts fat away. You think to yourself—"Hmmm, maybe I should buy shares of that stock before it goes up!" So in the excitement of the buzz, you sell stock you've been holding for a while and put it all in Fatgoz at $4/share. The next week you read in the paper that three people have died from the side-effects of Fatgoz, and when you check your stocks the next day you see that the shares are now down to $1.25 and what looked like a smart buy may be money down the toilet.

If your assets are substantial (that is, you have enough that if you lose a little you won't worry too much), you may want to think about setting aside 5 percent of your assets (in this case cash) as high-risk money, money you can spend on stock that is risky but if it DOES do well, you have the potential to make a lot of money. Risking more than 5 percent is a little like playing the horses at the race track or buying a lottery ticket every week. (Do you know the odds on ever actually WINNING the lottery?)

There is no magic age to start investing. But earlier is better, and today is not too soon. Wealth doesn't buy happiness. But it does offer options, and exercising your intellect and creativity to invest in your future is a secret not to be missed.

Irene and Sara concentrated on developing Sara's stock market savvy. The full collection of everything you invest in is called your "portfolio."

Irene convinced Sara over time, that although her collection of stocks was fun, it made sense to "diversify her portfolio." Investments tend to go up and down in cycles. If the cost of real estate is high when your stocks are low, or if your real estate is low and your stocks are high, you have some balance in your portfolio. Among other things that Sara began to add to her portfolio were:

⊙ *Insured savings deposits* (passbook savings, money market deposits, CDs) That is, she took some of her savings and made sure it was safe in a federally insured bank.

　　She wouldn't make as much on the money in these accounts, but if an earthquake struck or the market went to

> **Make Money While You Sleep**
>
> Compound growth is what happens when your interest pays interest.

the dogs, any money she had in these accounts would be insured. Even someone as willing to take risks as Sara could see the virtue in having a little safety net for some of her hard-earned money.

⊙ *Treasury bills, notes, or bonds* Irene also introduced Sara to what she thought was the safest investment: IOUs the U.S. government sells weekly to run its daily operations.

Treasury bills mature in a year or less; notes mature in one to ten years; and bonds mature (pay interest) in ten to twenty years. To find out how and where you can buy Treasury bills call the Federal Reserve Bank in Washington at (202) 452-3000, or check out the dollardiva.com site for another explanation of this kind of investment.

⊙ *Mutual Funds* This is another way to manage risk. Instead of having all your eggs in one basket so to speak, you may have your money invested in a fund that has 100 or more different stocks. Some may be up, others down, but on average, if the manager does the job right, over time the fund will provide a steady, if not terribly sexy, growth rate.

⊙ *Real Estate* At the age of 21, Sara wasn't ready to invest in real estate—though if she wanted to put her savings into a down payment on a condo and knew she would have income to pay the monthly mortgage payments, she could have rented it out while she went to college and had a small rental property. After a few years, she might have been able to sell the condo and have enough money to fund a couple of other dreams.

But real estate is a responsibility and Sara decided she wanted to focus on classes rather than the potential problems of tenants, so she decided to wait before putting her money into real estate.

The point is that what you invest in is personal. What works for Sara may not work for Irene. To invest is to choose the right combination of places to put your money so that it will grow in a way that suits you.

Some people will only put money into a fund that is virtually risk free. They may make less money, but they want to know they can count on what they have. Some people will only put money into companies that are women friendly; others won't invest in companies that aren't eco-sensitive.

And some people invest only in real estate, while others will only put their money in valuable paintings or stocks. Investments are as individual as the independent people who make them. The key is that they watch their money and feel responsible for turning it into more money they can use to make their dreams and the dreams of others come true.

Gear, Resources, and Actions for Investing

Check Out These Books

Beardstown Ladies Investment Club, Leslie Whitaker, Ed. *The Beardstown Ladies' Common-sense Investment Guide: How We Beat the Stock Market—and How You Can Too.* New York: Hyperion, 1995.

Card, Emily, Ph.D., and Adam Miller. *Busine$$ Capital for Women: An Essential Handbook for Entrepreneurs.* New York: Simon & Schuster, 1996.

Hunt, Mary. *The Financially Confident Woman.* Nashville: Broadman & Holman Publishers, 1997.

Orman, Suze. *The 9 Steps to Financial Freedom.* New York: Crown, 1997.

Schwab, Charles. *Charles Schwab's Guide to Financial Investment.* Reprint, New York: Three Rivers Press 1999.

Visit These Web Sites
www.dollardiva.com

www.financialfinesse.com

www.fool.com

www.thestreet.com

See These Videos
The Coca-Cola Kid, 1985.

Nine to Five, 1980.

Wall Street, 1987, (for what NOT to do).

Working Girl, 1988.

View on Television
MarketWatch, on CNBC

The Bloomberg Report

Thestreet.com

Read These Magazines and Papers
Business Week

The Wall Street Journal

Equity

Individual Investor

Try This

- Interview three certified financial advisors about what they do and how they do it.
- Start an investment club with 5–10 friends (See the *Beardstown Ladies Common-sense Investment Guide* for easy instructions on how to get organized.

$ecret

Defy Materialism

" You know that bumper sticker you see on Yuppie sportscars—'Whoever dies with the most toys wins!,' what I want to know is wins what?"
—Lynn G. Karlson

This next secret may seem confusing and contradictory. (Much about the independent life often is.) Having just been introduced to two secrets that encourage you to MAKE MONEY, why not assume that a companion secret would encourage you to indulge in an orgy of consumption? Buy till you die?

Big $ecret Four will offer part of the answer to this conundrum. But the truth is that if you are to be money conscious, you must also be conscious of your level of materialism.

Are things important to you? Do you equate who you are with what you have? Brazen materialists don't often wind up on the roster of DollarDivas—mostly because people who are really into "things" are by definition DEPENDENT. Dependent on their goods to tell them who they are. (So you're cool only if you have CK or DKNY initialed on your body?) Materialists are dependent on their things to tell the world they're important.

You have to be careful with things. I like my Manalo Blanik shoes a lot and feel very hot when I wear them to a gallery opening or a night on the town. But there's a difference between liking those shoes and being unable to do without them. Manalo rocks, but I'll be fine if I can't fill my closet with those shoes.

"Life is a series of trade-offs," my best friend, Jane, used to say. She meant if we were going to spend a lot of money on a great meal then we'd need to trade off indulgence somewhere else—like maybe staying at Motel 6 instead of the Ritz. Jane was right. Even where the option for flagrant consumption exists, exercising it may not be the best choice for the thinking Diva.

Anytime you buy anything, ask yourself:

1. Does what I buy undermine my goals to manage my money and build a long-term asset base? Will this purchase now prevent me from investing in something more important later? Or does this purchase mean I will not be able to make philanthropic contributions to causes I take seriously?

2. Does what I buy have an impact on human life? Is the item made in a country with a poor human rights record? Is the item made by women in sweatshops who put their lives at risk to produce it?

3. Does what I buy have an adverse impact on the planet? Does the making of this thing or the use of it, have some detrimental effect on the environment?

Sometimes it's tough to answer these questions, and companies with products to sell are savvy about "helping" you answer them. Buy this, and we'll donate $10 to the World Wildlife Fund or to the Hunger Project, their ads promise. (Don't buy it, and you can donate MORE to the WWFund or the Hunger Project yourself!)

Or, you may feel the urge to buy something because "it's made in America!" and you will be "supporting good labor practices!" (Good labor practices should exist, whether you buy or not.)

Navigating the waters of materialism, especially in America—and increasingly in other parts of the world—is hard work and requires the steel will of the confirmed independent, the woman who will make up her own mind about what she wants and needs, rather than cave to *(a)* peer pressure, *(b)* marketing mantras, or *(c)* her own fleeting impulses.

I find if I can walk away from something with the promise to myself that if I still want it in 24 hours I can go back and buy it, I usually forget the THING altogether. I'm a busy woman, I can't afford the TIME it takes to think about things constantly.

But when it comes to consuming travel, I admit, I'm slightly less careful and penurious. I recognize myself as an experience junkie, preferring to stock up on great memories than goods that gather dust.

Still, on the materialism scale, I'm probably a four, aspiring to be a three. Every now and then there is something so beautiful, so exquisite to look at, that I want to take it home with me. And though I typically shop the Gap outlet (and mostly hate shopping entirely, catalogs work just fine for me), when it's time to buy a nice jacket or pants I'll wear to important meetings, the clothes have to be on sale, but beautifully made.

I like the things around me to be chic for sure but I won't pay a fortune for stuff I can eventually track down at an estate sale for a fraction of the cost. When it comes to consumption of things: clothes, jewelry, or art, I'm patient, I can wait rather than pay too much for something I only kinda, maybe need.

The Material Girl's Scale

Level One

More is more. I define new. If I don't have it, it isn't worth having.

__ My friends count on me to lead the way on trends.

__ My idea of an afternoon well spent is spending money at the mall, buying new things.

__ I have to give things away or go to the thrift shop occasionally, just to make room in my closets for the new stuff.

__ I have the latest: handbag, shoes, earrings, CDs, Walkman, cell phone. I AM the latest.

__ My savings account is rarely higher than $50. What's money for, anyway?

Level Two

I'm not extravagant, but I don't deny myself either.

__ I may not be on the leading edge of every trend, but I have a dozen different kinds of nail polish and my CD collection is almost good enough for me to work as a rave DJ.

__ I love to eat out with my friends and chew my way through more cash than I save.

__ I'm very generous. Birthdays are an excuse to indulge my friends. And I do a lot of "one for her, one for me" shopping.

__ I only buy from companies that have good environmental policies.

__ I look for sales, but if I like something that isn't on sale, I'll buy it anyway; there's nothing wrong with buying retail.

Level Three

Less is more is my style. I'm a conscious consumer, but I slip occasionally.

__ I choose quality over quantity, and may save for a month to buy a sweater I really like, passing up three skirts that are great and on sale but that I don't need.

__ My friends sometimes accuse me of being a tightwad, but I won't spend money unnecessarily. (I may need new friends!)

__ I save money regularly, but only about five percent of whatever income I have, not the 10 to 15 percent I know I SHOULD be saving and investing.

__ I have a couple of good buying binges a year. Then I get a grip again.

__ I study labels and won't buy things that don't measure up to environmental or political values I hold.

Level Four

What's a trend? Stuff? Give me material for the mind.

__ I buy books, but I can't remember the last time I bought a jacket retail.

__ I save everything I can. I want to buy one of those new electric cars—they're so much better for the environment.

__ I like to eat out, but I can cook and often invite friends over to my house instead of stopping at the corner cafe with them.

__ I recycle EVERYTHING and am careful about what I purchase that can't be recycled.

__ I have school loans to pay for—nothing else is really important until they're paid off.

Level Five

I'm a prime candidate for an order of nuns who practice self-sacrifice.

__ There are very few things I want, and what I need I can get at the surplus store or a thrift shop.

__ Labels have no meaning to me, and I think people who pay for a label are pretty silly.

__ All things pollute in some fashion and I care more about the planet than I do about accumulation of things that harm it.

__ My savings account is pretty low; any money I have I give to the poor.

__ I do use the Internet, but I don't have the fastest connections, or the newest equipment. Speed isn't my thing, I'm patient.

So where do you fall on the materialist scale? You may have a different style every month. What's important is to be conscious of your style over time. It's unlikely that the long-term Level One Grrl is truly independent, a slave to fashion is by definition not much of a free thinker. But understanding your material self is one way to manage your money-self.

So what if you aren't sure you want to be a Level Five Consumer but do want to rethink your material needs and habits? You can do this. You can set trends, satisfy the odd craving, and manage your money-self, without entering an Order of Self-Denying Nuns (though that is an option). To reorder your consuming tendencies and reclaim your independent femme status, you only have to do the following:

1. Be aware of how you are manipulated.
2. Be clear on what choices you want to make.
3. Do your homework. (Have you noticed how often this comes up for the indie femme?)

4. Divide every dollar into three parts: part to save, part to give away, and part to spend.

Gear, Resources, and Actions for Defying Materialism

Check Out These Books

Stanley, Thomas J., and William D. Danko. *The Millionaire Next Door: The Surprising Secrets of America's Wealthy.* New York: Pocketbooks, 1998.

Twitchell, James B. *Lead Us into Temptation: The Triumph of American Materialism.* New York: Columbia University Press, 1999.

Visit These Web Sites

www.realsimple.com

Consumer's Almanac, **www.pueblo.gsa.gov/cic_text/money /almanac/calmanac.htm**

See These Videos

Trading Places, 1983.
Clueless, 1995.

Try This

Keep a journal of your consuming habits for a month. Notice your categories. In what do you indulge the most? Food? Clothes? Books?

Give Away Money

"Let it move through you ... because it creates space for more to come on in! Live and give with an air of generosity."
—Phyllis Lerner

Why on earth would you give money away???
Here's why some women do:

⊙ Katrina Garnett, the founder of Crossroads Software, wanted to encourage more high school women to pursue computer sciences. She gave away one million dollars to establish the Backyard Project, a program that does just that.

⊙ Cate Muther, a former vice president of Oracle Corporation, gave money to the Women's Technology Cluster, an incubator for businesses owned by women.

To "put yo   a big part of the
privilege and o   sider these issues:

- Pesticide
- Homeles
- Abandone
- Domestic
- Funding for
- Water pollut
- Relief efforts
- Medical resear   ncer, diabetes, and
  other diseases

Find Issues That Inspire You

What do you worry or care about? What issues concern you that
are NOT on this list? And what can you or will you do about any
of the world's problems that matter to you?

You have at least four big choices:

1. Ignore these big problems—they're too overwhelming
   for any one person to tackle.
2. Take time to get involved in one of the organizations
   already addressing ways to solve the big problems.
3. Give money to the people or organizations doing the
   hard work of making a difference.
4. Create your own solutions to the problem.

Don't Ignore the Big Problems

If you select option one, you might as well skip this section. This
secret will elude you altogether. One person can make a difference—and independent people know that.

In fact, one of the most motivating things you can say to some people is: "It can't be done." Some women who have chosen to tackle life's biggest problems include:

- ◉ Margaret Sanger, who dedicated her life to making sure women had the option of birth control.

- ◉ Rosa Parks and Jo Ann Robinson who, in 1955, went into action to change the policies of the Montgomery, Alabama, bus system that required blacks to get on the bus through the front door, pay for their ticket, then get off and reenter by the back door.

- ◉ Judy Chicago, the artist who organized an imaginary "dinner party" in 1979 by creating 100 plates representing women in history, bringing many of them "to the table for the first time and introducing them to the world."

- ◉ Ellen Malcolm, founder of EMILY's (**E**arly **M**oney **I**s **L**ike **Y**east) List. Ellen realized that the U.S. Congress did not have enough women representing the country and decided to do something about it by making sure that more women had the money required to run a successful campaign for the Senate or the House of Representatives.

- ◉ Rebecca Adamson, founder and president of First Nations Development Institute, an organization dedicated to helping Native Americans become more economically and culturally self-sufficient. A Cherokee raised in Ohio, she cashed her last unemployment check to pay for a fundraising trip to New York City. But her vision and persistence paid off: her first grant for the Institute was from the Ford Foundatin for $25,000.

These people shared a conviction that their actions could make a difference—even in the face of the greatest challenges life has to offer. The word "impossible" was not part of their vocabulary. Susan B. Anthony, who campaigned most of her life for a woman's right to vote—and who did not live to see the passage of the laws for which she struggled—was often heard uttering: "Failure is impossible." She was right.

But to make their efforts effective, each had to invest two things: time and money. And if they didn't have money themselves, they had to find other people who agreed with their cause and would support their ideas financially.

So we come to choices two and three: give time and/or give money. Historically, women who didn't have money gave their time to causes. In the United States especially, women created the phenomenon of the "volunteer" organization. If you needed something done and there wasn't any money to do it, you created an army of female volunteers. For centuries, women have organized benefit balls, cookie sales, and auctions. They have published cookbooks, written letters, made phone calls, and given millions of hours to make a difference.

Take Time to Get Involved

Giving your time, being a volunteer, and making a selfless contribution to the greater good of the community has come to be equated with being a good and virtuous person. But smart women know that change takes cash as well as time. Even if you have 100,000 people calling the U.S. Senate to push for strengthening environmental laws or marching to express outrage about chemical warfare or animal testing for cosmetics, it takes money to pay the telephone bills, put the marchers on buses, and buy the stamps for the letters to publicize the event. Whether it's the ability to pay rent on an office with someone to answer phones or to pay for the designer who creates the pamphlet that wrings the heart and changes the mind, money is one tool that every social activist needs.

So independent women may give their time to help make a difference. But these days, they also get involved by giving money.

Give Money and Create Solutions

Ah, but you're still relatively young and don't quite yet have a cool million laying around to give away? That's not important—giving money away is, as much as anything, a habit, a world view, and you can start practicing when you're 10 or 20 or 30. But sooner is better, and if you are 22 and haven't yet had the experience of giving some money away, there's no time like the present to start.

Remember that annual plan we talked about in $ecret Nine? That's where you add your vision for what problems you want to tackle and how you want to make a difference. Let's say you worry about the number of abandoned cats you see in your community. What can you possibly do to make a difference with regard to this problem? For starters:

- ⊙ Write a letter to the editor of your local paper, suggesting that he or she addresses the issue in the paper. This may cost you only 15 minutes, but could get the community talking.

- ⊙ Call or visit the local Humane Society and ask them what they are doing. Again, this may only cost you the price of a phone call or the time to visit the office. But once you have that information, you can volunteer time to spread the word or find homes for new kittens.

- ⊙ You may wish to donate money to have cats spayed and neutered. What can you afford for the year? Well, how much does it cost to have one cat spayed? Can you save that much in a year? Can you afford to give money to have five cats spayed? What if you were able to talk 10 friends into committing money from their "hamburger and Coke" allowance to each have five cats spayed? Ten friends times 5 cats each means you could affect the cat population by 50—now you're making a dent.

Five Ways to Give Away Money

You can make a difference by giving time, but you can also leverage—or extend the difference your time will make—if you can contribute money. So, giving money away is an important secret of DollarDivas. And if you start the habit of giving it away when you are young, it's a habit you will probably stick with all your life. So how do you give away money? There are five things you have to do.

1. Choose Your Issue or Issues

What do you care about? What issues have gotten you worried about the future of the planet or your community? In truth, you can't solve all the world's problems. But you can make a major difference in a few areas. Some people spend their entire lives tackling one great problem, others focus on two or three. The main thing is to "put your money where your mouth is."

If you are always going on about what a shame it is that people pollute the beach, or still wear fur coats, or don't house the homeless, but do nothing to help solve the problem, then you've got a big mouth, but not much power. Choose your target for making a difference, then get serious.

2. Do Your Homework

Who's already working on this problem? Do you want to get involved in an area that already has an army of helpers? Or do you want to get involved in a problem not receiving much attention? Social activists come in both stripes and both are important. It often takes an army of people and billions of dollars to solve some problems, so your contribution or effort, no matter how small, can add to the cumulative whole.

On the other hand, problems that are just whispers in the human psyche will need early flagbearers. Taking a risk to be the first to fund an unpopular issue or to speak out about a problem that others do not yet recognize takes courage and money.

Decide if you are an early money activist, or if you want to put time and money into issues that are clearly seen by many people as challenges to be met.

Then do your homework. Who else cares about the problem? This homework has never been easier with the aid of the Internet. Name the problem, and you can find any number of individuals who share your concern. But which of them are real and which are charlatans?! Who will really do effective things with your money and who will just line their own pockets by taking advantage of your heart's concerns?

Check out the two or three groups or individuals that seem to be doing the best work.

- ◉ Call them.

- ◉ Ask questions.

- ◉ Ask them to send you information about their organization.

- ◉ Ask for references. Speak with other people who have given them money, and see if they feel their money has been well spent.

- ◉ Find out how they report on their actions. Will you receive a letter every now and then telling you what has been done? Will they issue a report or must you request one?

- ◉ Is there a way for you to be involved by donating time, as well as money?

- ◉ Has the money they have received to date made any impact?

Once you are satisfied you have found an individual whose work you admire, or a reliable organization that you want to support you are ready to tackle the next step.

3. Add It to Your Annual Plan

Until that time comes when you have more money to give away than you need to live and survive, three to five percent of your annual plan is a reasonable amount to give away every year as a philanthropist. Let's say a cold look at your annual plan shows that you expect to have less than $200 this year from money earned in your yearly salary. Or maybe you're planning on $2,000 in income from a serious effort to build your client list, talk Aunt Mason into giving you cash instead of stationery for your birthday, and work out a deal with your parents to earn money for keeping the family car clean every month.

Five percent of $200 is $10 and 5 percent of $2,000 is $100. Both matter—remember if you only have $200 in income this year, what matters is that your vision includes money to give away. Next year you can build your income and watch as your 5 percent has greater impact.

4. Give the Money

You've done your homework, know where you want to donate the money, and have made your vision part of your annual plan. So write the check. (What do you mean you don't have a check book? Get to the bank and open an account!) Then send the money where it can go to do good work.

5. Follow Up

Don't orphan your money. Make sure it knows you care! Follow it to its new home and make sure it's well tended. If the donating organization doesn't send you a thank you card, doesn't give you a report on what they have done with your money at the end of the year, and simply treats you like a mother who has turned her child over to the state for care, fire them!

But if you think that your donation has been treated respectfully and that the people to whom you have entrusted it are making a difference, give them more the next year.

★   ★   ★

Don't be a short-term visionary—here today and gone tomorrow. Making change, making a difference, often takes a very long time. Women started working for the right to vote almost as soon as the Constitution of the United States was written and they discovered their voting rights had not been included. It was almost 150 years before they would see that fact changed and would be able to enter the voting booth legally—consider the patience and undying faith of the people who were the financial backers of that cause!

Unless you are completely uncaring about the world and your sister citizens, you will have an impulse to DO SOMETHING about the world's great challenges. You have tons of options.

Gear, Resources, and Actions for Giving Away Money

Visit These Web Sites
The Global Fund for Women, **www.globalfundforwomen.org**
www.giftaid2000.org.uk
www.dollardiva.com
Make-A-Wish Foundation, **www.wish.org**
www.giving.org

Subscribe To
Who Cares, The Tool Kit for Social Change, (202) 588-8920

Try This

- Survey your friends. Are any of them philanthropists? What do they care about? What do they contribute to?

- Create a list of 10 issues or causes you want to give money to. Start a journal and keep track of groups or opportunities where you can make a difference.

BIG $ecret Four:

Get Out of Yourself

You are important, special, and one of a kind. As a DollarDiva you are unique.

Now get over it! Once you thoroughly grasp your importance on the planet—you have to let go of it. The fact is, we're each unique, weird, and wonderful—and if you stay too wrapped up in your own drama, you'll miss the wonder around you.

Getting out of yourself is the special gift of the independent woman. Self-assured enough to recognize and include others, indie women reach out and pay attention to what's different in their own backyard as well as in the greater world beyond them. They care about something other than themselves.

Often people we admire most are least concerned about themselves (which is not to say they are careless about themselves). Their lives are interesting and admirable precisely because they have more going on than a perpetual interest in themselves—whether it's a dream they pursue, a passion that drives them, an insatiable curiosity about things around them, or a simple compassion for others. We like having these people around because they are more complex, interesting, and frankly, easier to be with.

$ecret Four, Get Out of Yourself, is a reminder that spending all your time learning only about yourself will make you a boring person indeed. Getting outside yourself has many dimensions: cultural, economic, political, and social. Practice the secrets in this section and become a deeper, more elegant version of the independent woman, a memorable DollarDiva.

13 $ecret

Cross Cultures

" To become an economically savvy independent Diva it is important to cross cultures. I grew up a lot after I attended Camp $tart-Up in the U.S., and made many American girlfriends. "
—Estefania Ossa from Argentina

At the end of the 20th century, Hollywood, NASA, and the Jet Propulsion Lab in Pasadena, California, did their best to remind us that we are all a speck in the eye of the universe. Tales of Armageddon, monster asteroids, erupting volcanoes, and flights to Mars helped us see the planet as a tiny, almost insignificant spaceship on which we are all, across countries and oceans, equally vulnerable.

At the same time that we were being made to feel small in the cosmos, our boundaries were stretched, our sense of "territory" challenged. Wall Street and the world press issued daily bulletins reminding us that we are in a global economy. The Internet made it possible to carry on friendships with people thousands of miles away as well as with those in the next town. World music emerged as a significant force on the music scene, and Prince Albert of Monaco started hosting the World Music Awards. MTV played in Mississippi and in Moscow. Schools began to offer Mandarin, as well as Spanish, for students wanting additional languages.

Political correctness and human decency conspired to include people of more diverse backgrounds in everything from advertising photo shoots and movie roles to the previously closed worlds of tennis and golf. And though the sworn enemies of affirmative action made it difficult, grass roots endeavors kept diversity a priority, and workplaces and educational institutions continued to hire and admit people for their skills and talent, as well as for the richness of their different cultures.

Now we can fax friends around the world in minutes and pass through cyberspace in an instant. The boundaries of the 'hood and the small town are forever broken. I stay in touch via e-mail with friends in Santiago, Chile; Sydney, Australia; and Anchorage, Alaska. My universe knows no bounds.

Whether you're in school with people from a multitude of races and cultures, in a workplace with people from diverse backgrounds, or play on a team with a motley crew, you have to be able to deal with difference today—if you can't, you aren't in the game, and independent women know this.

Still, hate crimes flourish, and though it is one thing to love the music of African musicians, develop a taste for Thai, or converse via e-mail with a kindred spirit in Calcutta, it is quite another to develop friendships with African tribeswomen, hang with those new neighbors who just immigrated from some country you can't pronounce, or date the person whose race and culture are so different from yours. But this difference is the special skill and secret of the independent woman.

How does one achieve a level of worldliness that allows you to walk in others' shoes, respect their cultures, be open-minded, and actually develop relationships that are deep and significant with people of vastly different cultures? How do we create bridges that can help span the chasms between our differences?

Ten Must-Dos to Cross Cultures

Ten must-dos to help with this challenge for the independent woman.

1. Think Local

Being cross-culturally sensitive is more than inviting an exchange student into your home or studying the mores of indigenous people around the world. In every community there are multiple groups of people, different by race, culture, or class—or by tradition. If there has been little contact between the groups, fear or wariness is likely to be the prevailing sentiment among them. Only contact can dispel notions of mutual weirdness.

The most useful contact is often found in some shared activity. How about building a house for Habitat for Humanity—(800) 334-3308)—and engaging churches in different parts of the community in the effort? Or maybe the local park could use a good cleanup—what better way to bring strangers together?

Whatever you choose, make it a real task, something that can transcend differences and help people experience common ground as they achieve something important. Lasting friendships and real relationships can evolve out of such activity—especially if these efforts are not one-shot deals but are sustained over time.

2. Explore Global

There are people who live in my town who never leave. For them, a trip to Los Angeles, less than 80 miles away, is as alien as a shuttle to the moon. They have conjured up L.A. to be just the way television and Hollywood films portray it: evil, corrupting, terrifying, and dangerous.

These people are not interested in testing that reality. They are all too willing to believe that the big city is a vile place—all the more reason to stay at home, nursing fears, believing stereotypes, and accepting the notion of the "outside world" as a place too awful to venture into.

Yet L.A., like all large cities, is filled with people who have dreams and aspirations. It is full of people who get up every morning ready to make the world a better place. Those people work against the stereotypes and the fears of others every day. And this is true around the world. It is not enough to form opinions about people and places based on reports from CNN, the local news, or word of mouth.

Exploring other cultures means setting foot in those cultures, examining up close what is real, separating rumor from reality. You can't expand your cross-cultural awareness fully until you actually cross into another culture.

3. Learn Languages

Have you ever gone to a movie with subtitles? Can you see how vastly different the experience of the movie is when you can't understand the nuances of the full dialogue? Slang, tone, and word choices all make language rich and meaningful. Language is a door. Unless you are fluent in more languages than your own, you can never fully enter another culture.

To point, nodding and trying to make yourself understood with only a few words, is to be like a three-year-old communicating with an adult—contact is made, but the depth of the relationship remains limited. Language may be the most important of all the skills of independence. If you cannot communicate directly across languages, you are dependent on others to translate—to give you THEIR version of what is being said.

In Australia, little children are enrolled in classes to learn Mandarin. Spanish, French, Italian, or German, whatever you choose—when you can immerse yourself in multiple languages you can truly immerse yourself in other cultures.

Fluency is not only a necessity of travelers and tourists. I once sat in the emergency room of a hospital in southern California. As I was waiting my turn, I overheard a nurse complain about those "stupid Mexicans" who wouldn't learn how to speak English. She was annoyed that it was hard to understand a Mexican family who had brought their little girl in for treatment and attributed the problem to stupidity, not to any shortcoming of her *own*—like failing to learn a modicum of Spanish so she might better deal with her clients!

As I sat there, I remembered the experience of my best friend, some years earlier, struck by an acute stomach problem while bicycling in Italy. Jane required hospitalization and found herself in a small facility where none of the medical staff spoke English. When she finally arrived home (safe and sound, happily) she told of how terrifying it was not to be able to communicate well with people who were about to examine her body.

I am always embarrassed when I cannot speak the language of people I suddenly encounter. It seems a major deficiency on my part not to make an attempt to learn basic phrases and words. I know that as an American in a Mexican hospital I would have limited ability to express myself. I hope the staff there would not simply call me stupid and write me off as unfit for treatment, but work with me to bridge the language gap. Fortunately, my friend received the treatment she needed. But medical emergencies aside, communicating in multiple languages is essential to one's ability to cross cultures.

4. Acknowledge Your Own Culture

You are a product of your own culture, making *you* strange and alien to others! It helps to be aware of who you are as a result of those cultural influences. Otherwise, it's all too easy to think of yourself as "normal" and everyone else as "different." Of course everyone is "normal" in their own world.

Get a handle on who you are, and you'll have a better appreciation of others. What do you eat regularly and why? What was your religious upbringing, if any? What holidays do you celebrate and why? What traditions or habits does your family practice that have shaped you?

I grew up in a rural part of the country. Most everyone in my part of the world was either Native American or American with European roots. I'm from Maine, where Downeast drawls are common. Every Saturday night we ate beanhole beans and brownbread.

Who I am has a lot do to with where I came from and the lessons I learned growing up. But I also observed how fearful people become when their culture isolates them, when everyone different seems alien instead of different and interesting. Only by understanding the ways in which our cultures shape us for good and bad can we transcend our culture and make connections outside our own insular communities.

5. Take Risks

There is a difference between feeling safe, and putting your head in the sand and pretending you're safe. Unless you explore "on the ground" instead of from your armchair or by watching the Discovery Channel, you will never truly experience another culture.

Most tourists miss the culture they spend good money and significant time to see, and that's the problem—they want to SEE, not experience. Checking off famous destinations from the window of a bus isn't the same as buying bread from the local grocer in a small Italian town, or working with villagers as a Peace Corps volunteer in the Andes.

And being reckless is not the same as taking risks, either. Crossing cultures is about building relationships, not daredevil adventure. Make sure you do your homework, learning as much as possible about the culture you want to enter, so you can be respectful about the rules and values of that culture.

The Business of Customs

Syndi Seid is the CEO of Advanced Etiquette. Based in San Francisco, it is the leading skills-building resource center in international business and social etiquette and protocol.

And what exactly does that mean? It means if you're going to school in Japan for three months, she can make life easier for you. Knowing how to be respectful of new friends and hosts is key to crossing cultural boundaries and Syndi Seid's business helps you learn customs and cultural givens BEFORE you make an idiot of yourself. Syndi is an independent woman who takes her work seriously.

"Independence carries with it the full weight and responsibility of being in total control of every aspect of my life," she says. "With every day that passes, I am required to make decisions and choices about EVERYTHING, from how I am going to spend my money, to where and with whom I am going to spend time and on, and on, and on.

"Traveling to other countries helped me learn a great deal about myself and how I choose to make these everyday decisions. By visiting other countries where the people do everything differently, from speaking to posture to eating, I've learned how necessary it is to be more accepting of others and appreciate how they may be different than me.

"I have learned to be much more tolerant, to investigate the origins of a person's behavior before criticizing it. I have learned to be more patient when someone does not understand what I am saying or trying to say. My discoveries all come from situations where I am the outsider, the foreigner."

6. Speak Out and Up

Have you ever stood by and laughed—uncomfortably—as someone told a racist joke? Have you failed to express disapproval when friends ridicule someone else because of their "difference"?

Being independent means sometimes standing alone against the crowd, and expressing an unpopular opinion. Independent people do not simply go along to get along. Racism and oppression can flourish only in an environment that tolerates them. The voice of one person, however tremulous, can shock a group's conscience back into operation. People may not be happy with

you for making them feel foolish, but you can remind them that
you are looking out for their best interests with this:

> In Germany, they came for the communists, and I didn't speak up be-
> cause I wasn't a communist. Then they came for the Jews, and I didn't
> speak up because I wasn't a Jew. Then they came for the trade unionists,
> and I didn't speak up because I wasn't a trade unionist. Then they came
> for the Catholics and I didn't speak up because I wasn't Catholic. Then
> they came for me—and by that time there was nobody left to speak up.
> —Pastor Marton Niemoller

7. Shut Up and Listen

Anxiety occasionally turns us into blithering idiots. When nervous, some people clam up, others can't keep quiet. If you feel
yourself sliding into a state where you have to talk to cover your
anxiety, chew gum. Nothing is more embarrassing to watch or
hear than the overanxious person protesting too much about how
"open-minded" he or she is.

To blather on about "my best friend who is [fill in the blank—
Asian, Black, Hispanic, white, and so forth]" or to go into a long
list of your "tolerant credentials" is humiliating. (I belong to . . . I
marched in . . . I am friends with . . .) If you really are at ease
crossing cultural boundaries, your actions will speak for themselves. If you are not comfortable when outside your cultural
comfort zone, shut up, listen, and learn.

8. Reach Out

Look around at your organizations, the clubs you belong to, the
swim team you practice with—does everyone look like you? Are
your social groups pretty homogenous? BORING! Fresh ideas,
invention, and possibility arise from ideas exchanged, fresh eyes,
and perspective.

If your social groups are homogenous, it's time to reach out
and bring in people who are different, people who reflect the diversity of the world around you. They will help expand the hori-

zons and possibilities of your group—and bring you into line with the real world.

Nothing annoys me more than hearing, "We *tried* to make the group more diverse but just couldn't find any [fill in the blank again: Asians, Anglos, Blacks, Whites, Hispanics]." If you can't find them, you're not looking. If you're not looking, you're not serious.

It's a simple matter, in this world, if you can't deal with difference, you can't deal with independence. Business, art, education—all life's most interesting pursuits—are fueled by the richness of diversity and difference. Out of the tensions of difference come creativity and learning.

It isn't easy—there is something extremely comfortable about staying with people just like yourself, like putting on jeans that are well worn in. But independent people don't just run with the pack; they lead, they explore, they include and reach out across invisible boundaries and habits.

9. Ask for Help

Suddenly you're in a group that has more diversity than you have ever experienced, and you can't breathe. You're afraid you'll say something wrong, stand out like a fool. Put it on the table.

Nothing helps like honesty. Seek out someone you trust and talk about your fears and your anxieties. Don't expect someone of a different race and culture to absolve you of the responsibility to make leaps across culture, but be open about the issues you have and listen to what they say back to you. Read. Knowledge helps. The more you know about the culture with which you are engaged, the greater your comfort level will be. Give it time: even in groups where people all look and sound alike, strangers or newcomers may be treated warily.

10. Find Personal Entry Points into Other Cultures

Immersion is a way to experience a culture as something other than a pure head trip. "Walk a mile in my shoes" is the challenge of really living another's reality. Exchange programs that put participants in the homes of families to learn a language or go to school provide their members one of the most effective ways to experience the day-to-day detail of a culture.

Living inside another culture is a way of discovering routines the host family takes for granted. But if you don't move to a village outside Quito or an apartment on the Left Bank, how else can you experience other cultures directly?

Face to Face with a New Culture

Estefania was 18 when she left her small town (population 20,000) in Argentina, to study business at the university in Buenos Aires. But she was more prepared than most young women for the experience of leaving home and learning to function in a new place because she had traveled abroad twice as a teenager.

Estefania's first trip outside of her country was to the United States, where she studied English at Phillips Academy Andover for three months. It was also, she writes, her "first [experience of] culture shock."

Much of Estefania's culture shock occurred while measuring the "real" USA against her very high expectations. The way she imagined the United States was not at all what she found, and this caused some confusion and homesickness. However, once she embraced what she did find, she learned a lot about herself and had fun, too. Estefania observed a number of cultural differences between the United States and Argentina. Sometimes she learned them the hard way!

The usual way of greeting people in Argentina includes kissing; Estefania once greeted someone in this fashion (after arriving in the USA), and felt quite embarrassed when she realized that it wasn't the usual custom. She also noted that people in the United States seemed very punctual and time-conscious in comparison to Argentinean folks.

Overall, examining differences and confronting the "real" USA was both interesting and important for Estefania, and this first trip abroad led to some serious independent thinking. She had to "resolve alone a lot of different situations" and think about cultural behavior and which country's customs she preferred.

Find something that matters to you and explore it in another culture. Shortly after the first democratic elections in 1990 in Chile, I became interested in helping to rebuild the public libraries in that country. Actually having a task to achieve gave me ample opportunity to experience another culture: how people work, their customs and habits, the values they hold dear.

But let's say your interest is music or dance. Attend performances, read about the history of the art in the culture of origin, or take lessons from people who learned the art from the generations before them. Volunteer in a community center that helps settle immigrants from other countries. No doubt you will teach much of your own culture, but you will also assimilate the new culture as well.

Independence is about knowing who you are—and understanding how that reality includes other people and other cultures. And the more you also understand that we are each a mere speck in the universe—diverse, divergent, and all one—the easier it will be to navigate that life as a worldly, aware, 21st century woman!

Gear, Resources, and Actions for Crossing Cultures

Try These Organizations/Visit These Web Sites
CIEE: Council on International Education Exchange
205 East 42nd Street,
New York, NY 10017-5716
(888) COUNCIL
www.ciee.org
Peace Corps Opportunities
(800) 424-8580
www.peacecorps.gov

STA-Travel
(800) 777-0112
www.sta-travel.com
The International Partnership for Service Learning
(212) 986-0989
www.studyabroad.com
Center for Cross-Cultural Study
1-800-377-2621
www.cccs.com

Read These Magazines

Transitions Abroad: The Guide to Learning, Living, and Working Overseas

Try This

Organize a conversation about diversity among your friends. Start by sitting in a circle and asking each person in turn to talk for no more than three minutes about what influence their family's cultural history has had on what they eat. Go around again and do the same thing with music, religion, values, etc. Not enough diversity among your friends? Add some new ones.

14 $ecret

Do Something

- Volunteer at a soup kitchen.
- Read stories to kids at the public library.
- Get a sculpture of a heroine erected in the local park.
- Organize a cleanup of a river bank or pond.
- Start a summer soccer camp for little girls.
- Wash a sick neighbor's car.
- Tutor in English, Spanish, math. . . .
- Intern at the Chamber of Commerce.
- Start a neighborhood watch.

" Whenever I find myself saying 'I can't,' it generally means 'I should' . . . and so I always do. Every risk you take opens at least two doors you never saw, all adding up to a path you couldn't have mapped out at the beginning of your journey."
—Martha Deevy

- ☉ Work with Habitat for Humanity and build a house for a low-income family.
- ☉ Visit elderly people at the nursing home or kids in the hospital.
- ☉ Organize a community garden or have a mural created for that abandoned building down the street.
- ☉ Start a Thanksgiving food drive for poor families.
- ☉ Organize a team to put a new coat of paint on the local women's shelter.
- ☉ Lead a campaign for better night lighting in the public park.

GET THE PICTURE? Do something that makes a difference for someone else. Independent people are blessed with the ability to make things happen precisely because they are independent. They dare to take stands, start things, cause trouble. Have you ever sat around with a group of friends and talked about how "someone" should take on a project. Make yourself that someone.

Independent people get outside of themselves by doing something for someone else. It is always curious how much comes back to us in the process, but that isn't the point. The point is to use your independent qualities to make a difference.

Volunteering

I'm always careful about urging independent women to volunteer. Too often volunteerism in the United States has caused women's labor to be exploited and unrecognized—contributing to the second-class economic citizenry of the world's women.

I do caution to make sure that your work is not unvalued and that volunteer work doesn't prevent you from developing a sense of economic empowerment. But assuming that you aren't giving away ALL your time and talent for free, it is important to make a contribution—to do SOMETHING for someone else that has no inherent reward other than making a contribution to the greater good.

Let's assume you are new to town or haven't been involved with anything outside of yourself yet. How will you get started? What can you do?

First Figure Out What Moves You

It makes no sense to read to kids at the library if the energy of little kids leaves you frazzled. And leading an environmental effort if your heart is dedicated to preventing cruelty to animals is a waste of passion. Let your heart speak to you and your actions will be all the more powerful. People have impact when they care deeply about the issue they are behind. Simply going through the motions doesn't count.

If you saw Martin Landau in the movie *Rounders,* you know what I mean. Landau played a wise law professor describing his early life studying to be a rabbi in Israel. He finally gave up that journey he said, to the despair and sadness of his family, because, "No matter how well I knew the Torah, I was never able to see the face of God." Explaining that he finally found his life's calling in the law, Landau was trying to make the point to the young man in front of him (portrayed by Matt Damon) that it doesn't matter how well you do something; if your heart is not engaged in the pursuit, you will always be cheating yourself and the goal.

Second, Find Out What Needs to Be Done

If everyone in town is raising money to build a new library, but the animal shelter is falling apart, the animal shelter probably needs you more than the library does and may be a better place to invest your time and energy.

To figure out what the needs are, talk to people, walk around the community, and see what YOU think is needed. Then ask who needs what. It's amazing how many "good works" are done that aren't needed! For example, the kids in the neighborhood may have no place to play—but some well-intended do-gooder decides to plant flowers along the sidewalk.

Did anyone say they wanted more flowers along the sidewalk? Maybe not. If asked, they might have said they needed a bike path for the kids or a hospice for AIDS patients. You don't really get outside of yourself unless you ask others what their needs are rather than giving them what you think they need.

People are funny. Sometimes good works happen because people want to see their names in the newspaper. ("Jay Freeman honored for giving the most hours to the local children's theater workshop," or "Park Named After Hospital Patron.") But doing something outside of yourself means doing something that NEEDS to be done because it needs to be done—not because you need recognition.

Third, Get Organized

Once you've identified a need that is connected to something you care about, find out who has already been working on the problem and offer to lend a hand. If you really want to help (as opposed to just taking charge), you'll find out who has already made some relevant effort, what they learned, and what they think is needed.

For example, maybe you've heard there are no green spaces in a neighborhood and that the community won't allow neighbors to use abandoned lots to start a community garden. Are you going to go to City Hall demanding something be done? Probably not until you find out if anyone else has been to a meeting with the city planner and discussed the problems. Probably not until you find out if any leaders in the community already have a plan in place.

Independent women can be dangerous! Just because we ARE independent doesn't mean we should or need to always be in the lead or work alone. Finding out who you can work with and what the lessons have been to date will make your efforts all the more valuable.

Fourth, Leverage Your Efforts

This is a place where independent women can seriously make a difference. Use your ability to develop a vision to make a BIG difference. For example: if there aren't enough volunteers to help care for the animals at the local shelter, you can sign yourself up for a few hours a week and a couple of animals will be better off for it.

But if you recruit 10 friends and sign them each up for three hours per week—you can "**leverage your impact**!" With a vision that extends beyond yourself, you can go from helping a few animals two or three hours per week to making a difference for a lot of animals for 30 or more hours every week.

Extend that vision again—is there more than one shelter in your city? Can you get friends to each "adopt a shelter" and schedule volunteers every month? Don't be afraid to think big—if a need exists, it probably exists in a big way and may need big solutions. Indie women are unafraid of large-scale problems and large-scale solutions. Leveraging impact is great experience for solving other problems you will face in your life!

Take Initiative

What if you identify a problem no one has been willing to tackle yet? Then it's probably a need that, like an orphan, requires you all the more. Just because no one has ever undertaken a problem before is no reason you can't grapple it. There is no age limit—high or low—on the ability to reach outside of yourself to *do something!*

Especially if you have declared that "the emperor wears no clothes" by identifying a problem no one wants to deal with, you will hear such objections as: "That's just the way things are, you can't change that." "Oh, that's not really a problem." "You're too young to do anything about that." "Eventually, that problem will take care of itself." "We're already working on this."

All of these responses are, of course, strategies for maintaining the status quo—in other words, keeping things the way they are. Fortunately, really independent femmes are rarely distracted by these paltry defenses. If something needs to be done, an indie grrl will find out why it isn't being done and make something happen.

Almost every need requires funds. (Better review Big $ecret Three: Grow Your Money-Self for this—in the end, economic power is a factor in almost everything you want to do.) Let's say that you notice that there are fewer and fewer old trees on the streets of your town. Somehow they are simply disappearing, and no one else seems to notice.

What's going on here? Is a disease killing them off? Is the city taking out old trees to put in new cable wires? Are they being replaced by wider streets for cars?

If you miss the trees and think people are making short-term decisions that are bad for your town, what can you do to attract people's attention? Of course, first you do your homework. Check to make sure your perceptions are real and not just flights of your imagination.

How many of those elm trees were on the streets five years ago? How many today? Who can tell you what happened to those trees? Maybe a conversation with the head of your Parks and Recreation Department at City Hall can tell you. Or if there's a local chapter of the Audubon Society, maybe they will know, because fewer trees certainly means fewer birds. Once you know the real numbers and the cause of the decline, you have ammunition to make your case. And now you may also know who you can enlist to help you out—and who has MONEY!

If the cause is a disease that the city planners say is too expensive to treat, you need to talk to tree experts at a university who might have a solution. By informing the head of the Audubon Society about the options, you might find someone willing to advance some new ideas—and find funds to deal with the issue. Or if fewer trees are the result of wider roads and new traffic plan de-

signs, you might want to engage the help of a real-estate professional who will argue that streets without trees will lower the
value of city homes. They may have ties to organizations that can
contribute money to fund the fight.

Doing something almost always means figuring out who your
natural allies are and offering solutions that will unhinge your op-
ponents. Big problems are rarely solved because they SHOULD
be, but because there is enough compelling evidence or a ground-
swell of support for change. You can be the catalyst for both.

Causing Ripples

A catalyst, like a chemical agent, causes change, or starts a process
whose effects are not always calculated. You can almost never do
something without causing ripples. Like a stone in a pond, any
action you take, anything you do, will create waves, make
changes. You have to be thoughtful, because not all ripples are
good ones. But doing something will necessarily have consequences.

Let's say you do decide to visit a lonely woman in a nursing
home once a week. You may see things you think need improve-
ment there: the food they are fed, the kind of activities offered—
or the lack thereof. These observations can take on a life of their
own and cause a stir. And not all of those ripples will make
people happy. The nursing home may see you as a troublemaker if
you don't just visit the client and then leave. Or other patients
may be concerned that issues you raise will be taken out on them.
When you do something you have to be aware of the consequences of your actions. Note I said aware, not afraid.

The miracle of having independent women do something is
that when ripples occur—good and bad—they are there to deal
with them. Women who have really incorporated Big $ecret
One: Accept Yourself are prepared to do things without asking

permission; they take their ideas and passions and goals seriously and act on them—and they get **LOUD** when they need to. In some ways, Big $ecret Four depends on mastering Big $ecret One. And if you haven't taken care of Big $ecret Two: Uncover Yourself, you may not know what really moves you—what you care about and are willing to take a stand on. In the end, as you can see, all the secrets are critical to making a difference when it's time to DO SOMETHING.

Gear Resources and Actions for Doing Something

Check Out These Books

Brooks, Susan M. *Any Girl Can Rule the World*. Minneapolis: Fairview Press, 1998.

Karnes, Frances Ph.D., and Suzanne M. Bean, Ph.D. *Girls and Young Women Leading the Way: 20 True Stories about Leadership.* Minneapolis: Free Spirit Pub., 1993.

Try These Organizations

Amnesty International
(202) 775-5161

www.amnesty-usa.org

The Echoing Green Foundation
(212) 689-1165

www.echoinggreen.org

Students for the Exploration and Development of Space
MIT Room W20-445
77 Massachusetts Avenue
Cambridge, MA 02139
(888) 321-SEDS

www.seds.org

Visit These Web Sites

Youth Leaders International

www.leaders.org

Project America

www.project.org

www.ottermedia.com

This is Julia "Butterfly" Hills' official Web site. Julia lived in an ancient redwood tree for *two years* in order to save it!

Read These Magazines

Do Something

Who Cares

Try This

1. Think of two things that you would like to have done for yourself . . . and then do them for someone else.
2. Think of two ways you could implement a small change in yours, or your family's lifestyle that would benefit the environment:

⊙ You could develop and institute a new recycling program in your household.

⊙ Come up with a more efficient way to car pool.

⊙ Organize a local cleanup group, i.e., beach, park, city streets, mountainside

$ecret 15

Vote

" When you don't bother to vote, don't be bothered by the way things are. "

—Lizzy Rao

Do you know what kind of voting record your Senator or Representative has that affects you? (Do you know who *your* Senator is?)

What if you discover that he or she consistently votes against any bill that would create more jobs for teens, funding for after-school programs, or for college scholarships? What if you find that he or she consistently votes for curfews, stiffer penalties for minor offenses, and harsh treatment for teen moms? Are you going to stand for that?

Consider the case of two Kentucky High School seniors about to be elected into the National Honor Society. Chastity Glass and Somer Chipman both had grade averages of 3.5. But the school's honor society chapter refused to induct them because they were pregnant but not married. The Society (or whatever fuddy-duddies were in charge) said they didn't want the young women because the chapter wanted to "encourage high morals and strong character."

The two young women showed their strong character by seeking to change the vote. Enlisting the help of the American Civil Liberties Union, they sued the society and in December of 1998 a federal court ordered the society to accept them.

Chastity Glass went on to attend Morehead State University and said of the victory: "I feel I was left out unjustly. This was a very big deal to me, to be treated the same as my peers." This indie woman understood how to use the political process to undo a vote that affected her life in a very powerful—and negative—way.

MTV started "Rock the Vote" in 1994, and teenagers began to pay attention to the impact of politics on their lives. You can't vote in a national election until you are 18, but you can affect the political process. If you don't, you and your pals will be rolled over like so many ants under a Harley tire. Indie women don't ignore the political side of their lives.

Indie women get hip, read, pay attention to who is in office, listen to what is being said by politicians and policy makers—and if they don't like what they see or hear, they GET LOUD, use their economic muscle to remove those politicians from office, and they *do something* to effect change. (See how each $ecret leverages the impact of the others? When you have them all under your belt you will be mighty powerful and independent indeed!)

How to Register to Vote

Where can you register to vote?

By phone:
Call 1 800 345 VOTE
1 800 232 VOTA (in Spanish)
to receive an application by mail

By internet:
www.govote.com
This site allows you to download an application online. Be careful though, because some states do not accept this application.
www.rockthevote.org
This site also allows you to apply for a registration card and is also a great resource on political issues.

In person:
A registration application may be obtained from the local election officials in your county. You can also register to vote when applying for services at State DMV and drivers' licensing offices.

How to Be Involved in More Ways Than Voting

19th Amend- ment

Adopted in 1920. The right of citizens of the United States to vote shall not be denied or abridged by the United States or by any State on account of sex. The Con- gress shall have power to enforce this article by ap- propriate legis- lation.

Vote Anywhere, Anytime You Can

You can have impact on many levels. Vote on your city council. Too many decisions are made by just a few people who show up and vote. By ignoring this simple, vital act—an act that good women and men have lost their lives to attain—you ignore your most powerful tool. Getting in the habit of voting whenever you can is like flossing—you will do it for the rest of your life.

Influence Other People's Votes

Lots of people are just too lazy to gather the facts about issues or people to be voted on. (This is never the case for the truly inde- pendent woman.) These lazybones are easily influenced by other people's ideas and information.

So get your information and news in front of people who will vote: college friends of voting age, parents, grandparents, friends of the family, teachers. Create a flyer with information that sup- ports your view, and hand it out. Send e-mail messages with in- formation about a vote. Get together with your friends and compose a message to air on your local public access station.

Set up a press conference and invite local (or national) press to cover your story. (So you think only celebrities can do a press con- ference? What do you think made them famous in the first place?)

Encourage Other People to Vote

It's astonishing how many people who CAN vote, don't or won't bother. They're either lazy, stupid, or simply tuned out. It's your responsibility to get them tuned in (hopefully to your point of view, but at least to the act of participating in the community). This is an easy thing to do. Guilt is an effective tool, so is anxiety. And if you have information at hand you can wield both weapons to get people off the couch and into a voting booth.

Guilt: Tell anyone you know who doesn't intend to vote what a bad role model he or she is. They should be ashamed. If that doesn't work, step up the heat. Don't they care about the future? If they don't vote, they will put the future at risk. If that still doesn't work, you could threaten to let everyone in the family know they didn't vote, leaving them open to embarrassing comments and stares. And as a final tactic, offer to drive people to the polls.

Anxiety: This sometimes works when guilt doesn't, but it requires more research. You have to discover the issues that DO matter to them and find out which candidate will vote against their wishes. For example, your uncle owns a sailboat; he loves to sail in the summer in a large lake about three hours from his home. You find out that one of the candidates wants to pass a law exempting all motorboats from any safety requirements on that lake, meaning that the quiet lake your uncle has been enjoying will now be filled with loud boats zooming around him. If he stays home and doesn't vote, he'll have a direct hand in destroying his own summer pleasure! Or let's assume your sister in college is "too busy to vote." Her midterms are looming and she doesn't want to take the time to cast a ballot. Would it make a difference if she knew that her right to privacy with her doctor was about to be taken away with a local ballot initiative? Maybe, but if she isn't paying attention to the political process, she won't know.

Indie women are always vigilant about what they realize they don't know. Only by staying on top of the political process can you know what kind of tricks some cagey group with a plan of their own may be about to play on your life.

Use the Strategies of Civil Disobedience

(You'll find $ecret Three comes in handy on this one!) Anyone who has been disenfranchised or oppressed has encountered times when civil disobedience is a moral requirement. When laws or customs are used to harm the rights of others, sometimes the only way to bring about change is by following the traditions of civil disobedience: a silent vigil in front of an office building of the politician who voted against funding the women's education center; marches protesting the firing of a beloved teacher who went against outdated school policy.

Volunteer for a Politician Whose Point of View Is in Line with Your Values and Goals

Anyone running for office counts on the energy and intellect of an army of young people who will do anything—answer phones, make phone calls, stuff envelopes, go-fer coffee, go-fer office supplies, post campaign posters—that will get that candidate and his or her point of view before the voting public. Putting your energy to work for someone who will vote on issues that matter to you, in the manner you want, is one of the most effective ways to use your talent to DO SOMETHING. It's great work experience and can also be a stepping stone to another job—who knows, you may decide to run for office yourself someday. Which brings us to . . .

Run For an Office

Whether it's a seat on the city council, a seat on the board of trustees for college, or the board of a company, you can show your independence and exercise VOICE (see $ecret Four: Get Loud) by being a part of the decision-making body that effects change and policy.

Voting = Independence

Voting, affecting other people's votes, or being the candidate on the ballot are all elements of democracy that people all over the world cherish, fight for, and grieve for when they are lost. Independent women understand that their independence has been won *because* they can vote, because other women fought for the right to vote—and if it is undermined in any way, the independence they need, like breath itself, will be at risk.

Look at what you have as a result of voting:

- ⊙ The right to vote.
- ⊙ The right to attend school.
- ⊙ The right to hang with your friends—anytime, anywhere. (In some communities this is limited by curfews and other local laws intended to reduce teen violence.)
- ⊙ The right to speak your mind.

Now imagine this scenario: It is the year 2012. The right to vote has been restricted to men over 40 with black hair. Suddenly everyone else has to live under laws that are made by and enforced for men over 40 with black hair. These are guys who like their dinner on time and want everyone else to live in dorms so they can live in peace and not be bothered with having to SEE anyone who doesn't look, think, or act like they do.

They also pass a set of laws barring under-forties who are not black-haired males from going to school, shopping in malls, and going to any public entertainment. (Concerts and movies are off-limits.) They dictate a uniform that is used by everyone who is not like them and decide what work is done by whom at all times.

Because we have squandered our natural resources, fresh fruits and vegetables are now rare, clean water is more precious than diamonds used to be, and as a result the under-forty folks who are not black-haired males can only drink murky, recycled water and eat fake vegetables made of soybeans.

The land has been mined and developed in such a way that only small perfect islands of unblemished villages and beautiful vistas exist—and are off-limits to all but the chosen few.

Fantastic? Let's hope so. Let's hope this is the stuff of bleak science fiction and nightmares that come late at night. But abdicating one's right to vote is a signal that you don't understand the importance of your voice and your values. It's a sign that you are willing to allow a few people to impose their vision on the world. Claim your right to vote and to affect votes; it's part of your heritage as an indie woman.

Gear, Resources, and Actions for Voting

Check Out These Books
Atwood, Margaret. *The Handmaid's Tale.* New York: Anchor Books, 1998.

Cain, Bruce, Morris P. Fiorina, and John A. Ferejohn. *Personal Vote: Constituency Service and Electoral Independence.* Cambridge, Mass: Harvard University Press, 1987.

Fritz, Jean. *You Want Women to Vote, Lizzie Stanton?* New York: Putnam, 1995.

Wheeler, Marjorie Spruill. *One Woman, One Vote: Rediscovering the Woman Suffrage Movement.* Troutdale, OR: NewSage Press, 1995.

Visit These Web Sites
Youth Speak, **www.oblivion.net/youthspeak**

www.rockthevote.org

See These Videos
Votes for Women
Ishtar Films
15030 Ventura Blvd., Ste. 766
Sherman Oaks, CA 91403
(800) 428-7136

Try This

1. Organize a coalition on your school campus, or church, or in front of the supermarket to encourage voter registration.
2. Volunteer your time, energy, and creativity for your favorite political cause.
3. Engage three people whom you respect in conversation about their political views concerning a topic of interest to you. You could be surprised by what you may learn.
4. Join the debate team.
5. Volunteer time for a political candidate or committee you support.

$ecret 16

Mind Your Manners

" Be careful of the things you say to others. You can always be forgiven, but you can never take it back."

—Helen Kenney Elliott

This is completely ridiculous, but utterly necessary. One assumes that everyone understands good manners—but there are few enough gracious, independent divas, that it's clearly a secret many miss. The greats do not.

No one likes to embarrass herself and though (almost) everyone knows that belching at lunch is a sure way not to be invited back for a second round of interviews, not everyone is aware of the tiny ways we can sabatoge our best opportunities. Manners are a way of signaling respect, worldliness, and a certain level of elegance.

7 Dangerous Situations in which to Be Stuck with Bad (or No) Manners

1. Meeting your boyfriend's parents for the first (or fourth) time.

2. Going for a job interview. Going for the second job interview.

3. At a bar.

4. Having dinner with new friends.

5. On an airplane.

6. At the Olympics.

7. On the *Tonight Show*.

You can act any way you want all the time. That's one of the prerogatives of the independent woman. (Who cares what anyone else thinks, right?) But there's a difference between acting any way you want and not knowing how to act. If you are ambushed by Howard Stern the next time you're on his radio show and he asks an embarrassing question you do NOT want to answer but don't know how to avoid deftly—you will be on the defense.

If, on the other hand, you have a repertoire of behaviors based on good manners, or decent etiquette, you can squeeze out of any slippery situation with grace and elegance—*holding the upper hand at all times.* Let's examine the dangers lurking in the seven situations listed below.

Meeting Your Boyfriend's Parents

Let's assume for a moment that this relationship is more than a fleeting fancy and you really want them to like you. In fact, there has been talk of the family taking a long trip to Europe next summer and there is a chance they might include you. The stakes are high.

SCENARIO ONE (NO MANNERS MADELINE MEETS MOM AND DAD)

MOM AND DAD: Hi, Madeline, nice to meet you. How are you?

MADELINE: Ummm, uh, fine I guess. (Silence.)

MOM AND DAD (reaching their hands to shake Madeline's): Well, it's nice that you could join us. Won't you have a seat?

MADELINE (ignoring the hands held out to her): Yeah, sure. (Takes seat, slouches. Silent.)

Mom and Dad are already thinking: "She's pretty mousy, what does our son SEE in her? She'd be awful to take to Paris with us."

SCENARIO TWO (MADELINE MINDS MANNERS)

MOM AND DAD: Hi, Madeline, nice to meet you. How are you?

MADELINE: Fine Mr. and Mrs. Adams. (Reaches out to give a firm handshake.) Thanks for inviting me here today.

MOM AND DAD (shaking Madeline's hand): Well, it's nice you could join us. Won't you have a seat?

MADELINE: Thank you. Tom has mentioned the work you do in the community, and I've been eager to hear more about it.

Mom and Dad are already thinking: "How gracious, she'd be a great addition to the Paris trip next summer."

It happens that quickly. Impressions and decisions are made in less time than it takes to tie your running shoes. Sometimes you can recover—but not always—and why take the risk? You can be as laid back and informal with your friends and Mr. and Mrs. A's son as you want to be, but when meeting strangers who have nothing on which to base their impression of you but those first speed-of-light seconds, you have to be wary of the conclusions they will draw about you. If you want life to be smooth with their son, don't make it hard for him to defend you!

You think such shallow first impressions are unfair? Maybe they are, but that's how life is, and you can either use your repertoire of good manners to make a good impression or you can risk it all by "being who you are" at all costs.

The Job Interview
SCENARIO ONE (NANCY HAS NO CLUE)

NANCY RICE, JOB CANDIDATE: Hi, I'm here to see Ms. Wild about the job you advertised.

RECEPTIONIST: Ms. Wild has been delayed, if you will take a seat and wait, she'll be with you as soon as she can.

NANCY RICE: Jeez, she *said* two o'clock, and I'm here now. . . . Who does she think she is, anyway?

RECEPTIONIST (patiently): She had a family emergency and will be with you as soon as possible.

NANCY RICE sits for a few minutes, fidgets, poking around in her handbag, puts on her Walkman and earphones and keeps time with her tunes. MS. WILD returns and the RECEPTIONIST goes to her office to announce the job applicant: "Well, the applicant is here, but this will be quick for you, she's a real piece of work."

SCENARIO TWO (NANCY KNOWS WHAT TO DO)

NANCY RICE, JOB CANDIDATE: Hi, I'm here to see Ms. Wild about the job you advertised.

RECEPTIONIST: Ms. Wild has been delayed, if you will take a seat and wait, she'll be with you as soon as she can.

NANCY RICE: Thanks, no problem. While I'm waiting, do you have anything I can read about the company to give me more background? I've been looking forward to this interview for days.

RECEPTIONIST: Well, there's an annual report on the coffee table you might find interesting.

NANCY RICE (reads quietly, then puts the report down): Thanks, I appreciate having this information. Would it be easier for Ms. Wild if we rescheduled?

Just at that moment, MS. WILD returns and the RECEPTIONIST goes to her office to announce the job applicant: "This applicant seems really thoughtful and considerate—I think you'll enjoy her."

Once again the impression made is instrumental in other's decisions about you—and once again it occurs in small and subtle ways. Never assume anyone in a company is unimportant or will not report on your behavior. For all you know, that receptionist is the daughter of the company owner, simply working her way up the ladder. Grace and patience pay off when you spread them around liberally and with good manners.

At the Bar

This could be a water bar, a wine bar, or the smoothie bar—what is imbibed is much less important than what goes down.

SCENARIO ONE

BERYL and BEVERLY stop by a new bar on their way home from work. It's crowded, but they see three stools at the bar. The two of them sit down and place their coats and briefcases on the third stool. After a few minutes, a woman comes over and asks if they would move their coats so she and her companion might sit. The two give her a sneer and tell her to find another seat. The woman is surprised at their lack of generosity, but walks away. They can see the woman and her companion standing uncomfortably by the door, but ignore them and continue with their conversation.

The next morning, the two arrive at the weekly staff meeting and discover the person they treated so rudely the night before has just been hired as the new district manager. She will have responsibility for their promotions and salaries!

SCENARIO TWO

BERYL and BEVERLY stop by a new bar on their way home from work. It's crowded, but they see three stools at the bar. The two of them sit down and place their coats and briefcases on the third stool. After a few minutes, a woman comes over and asks if they would move their coats so her companion might sit. They immediately pick up the coats and wave to her to please use the seat. She thanks them and mentions she's new in town and has just been hired at a local company. "It's nice to see people in this new town are so gracious," she says.

The next morning, the two arrive at the weekly staff meeting and discover the person they treated so kindly the night before is the new district manager they had heard about. She mentions that he has already met the two of them and was delighted to have such a warm welcome her first night in town.

Wild coincidence? Maybe. But coincidences happen all the time. And the person you "dis" today may be the person you need tomorrow. Manners pay off in hard cash and opportunity sometimes.

Having Dinner with New Friends

SCENARIO ONE

It's your first year in New York City, and your roommate has invited you to join her and some of her friends for dinner. You meet them at an Italian restaurant for pizza and conversation. When you arrive, the six of them are laughing and talking. Your roommate introduces you and ten minutes later you are regaling them with stories about your college days. Twenty minutes later you're still going on and continue talking, right through the last piece of pizza.

Three weeks later you ask your roommate if you can join her again. She hesitates, then lets you have it. "They thought you were pretty funny at first, telling all those stories, but when you continued talking with your mouth full—never stopping to ask them anything—they decided you were boorish and boring. I think you'd better find your own friends to eat with."

SCENARIO TWO

It's your first year in New York City, and your roommate has invited you to join her and some of her friends for dinner. When you arrive, the six of them are laughing and talking. Your roommate introduces you. When you find the chance you ask them a question and they start to talk about things you have in common. When the pizza arrives, you are careful to answer questions and tell stories when you've finished a bite, or when everyone has taken a break while laughing about someone else's story.

Three weeks later, you've become a regular member of the group, joining them often for dinner.

If no one at home ever told you how disgusting it is to watch someone eat with her mouth open, you may discover the hard way. I once had an employee whose food habits were so bad I often excluded her from any luncheon meeting during which she might embarrass her teammates and the company.

New friends have a choice—they can exclude people from the circle who talk incessantly, with no curiosity about others, or who have such bad eating habits that it's hard to be at a table with them. Unless you want to eat alone all the time, minding how you handle your food and your mouth is a key element of manners and menus.

On an Airplane

I have never seen a video or a book that tells people how to behave on a plane. But there are rules. And independent women who are frequent travelers know them. It's sort of the ESP of travel. When you break the rules, you look silly and amateurish and are treated that way.

SCENARIO ONE

This is not your first time on a plane, but you are really excited. You're sitting in the middle seat and, before the plane takes off, you crawl across the person on the aisle twice: once to go to the bathroom, once to get a magazine. When you finally sit down and have your seat belt locked, you fish in your purse for the bubble gum you bought earlier and start blowing bubbles. You've heard it's good for ear pressure.

As soon as the plane is in the air you start to talk to your seat companions. You ring your call button for the flight attendant. The person on your left reminds you that the attendant can't come until the seat belt light goes off, but you press it again, like an impatient cabbie honking his horn on Madison Avenue. Though both seat companions have books and seem to be reading, you continue to ask them a lot of questions about where they are going, what they do, and tell them who you are and where you are going.

Finally the passenger on your right gives you a hard stare and asks you to please be quiet. The one on your left puts on the ear phones and ignores you completely. And for the rest of your 18-hour flight to Australia, the flight attendant finds all kinds of reasons to ignore you.

It's the Little Things that Count

Elissa Cruz graduated from Camp $tart-Up in 1999. One of the classes that struck her was the Power etiquette course in which the power of posture was stressed. "Sit and stand straight and tall" the class was reminded, "and people take you more seriously."

When invited to be interviewed for the Fox Channel, producers of the show were struck by Elissa's poise and posture. And they offered her a modeling job!

SCENARIO TWO:

This is not your first time on a plane, but you are really excited—you will be spending a month working as a consultant in Australia. You are sitting in the middle seat, so before you sit down you go to the bathroom and make sure you have all the reading materials you want in your hand. You bought some gum and are chewing it discreetly because you know it can ease air pressure on your ears.

Before the plane takes off, you introduce yourself to your seatmates and then open a book and begin to read or listen to tunes with the earphones. But it's a long flight, and when you have to get up later to go to the bathroom, you excuse yourself and give the passenger on the aisle plenty of time to move before getting up.

A few hours before the plane lands, one of your seatmates asks what you will be doing in Australia, and you explain. Very interested in your plans, she invites you to dinner in the outback where she manages a large ranch.

Airplane manners are tricky; no one tells you what they are, you are expected to pick them up by watching others or by being made to feel foolish a few times. But there's no mystery to how to be patient, quiet, and observant—you can quickly tell the amateur from the experienced flyer. And independent women who spend time on planes are rarely amateurs. Planes are great places to meet new people and have new doors opened, but you have to be gentle about intruding on their very limited space!

At the Olympics

You are probably thinking, "What are the chances I'm going to the Olympics?" Okay, so maybe not. But you *will* be in an international group of people at some point—and whether it's the Olympics, a meeting of international choral singers at a music festival, or a soccer meet with the championship team from Brazil, you will need to know something about customs outside your 'hood.

SCENARIO ONE

You are a champion gymnast, and you've just arrived at the Olympic Village and are looking for your room. As you enter the reception area, you see someone you assume is another competitor.

CHAMPION GYMNAST: Hey, where can I put my things? Where's my room?

The STRANGER responds in a language you don't recognize.

CHAMPION (muttering): What an idiot, she doesn't know anything.

Just at that moment the VILLAGE HOST steps up, asks for your ID, and says, "The person you just called an idiot is one of your judges and may not speak your language well, but certainly understands it."

SCENARIO TWO

You've just arrived at the Olympic Village and are looking for your room. As you enter the reception area, you see someone you assume is another competitor.

CHAMPION GYMNAST: Hey, where can I put my things? Where's my room?

The STRANGER responds in a language you don't recognize.

CHAMPION: (Holds out hand to shake and says, quietly,) "Sorry, I am Jane Jackson, from the United States. And you are?"

The STRANGER responds, giving her name, and says that she is from Sweden. In her own language she remarks that she is happy to meet an arriving athlete. Just at that moment the VILLAGE HOST steps up, asks for an ID, and translates the message just given to you and says, "This is is one of your judges, she understands your language well, but is shy about speaking it, she appreciates your patience."

When in an unfamiliar situation, make no assumptions about who speaks what, what they understand, or who they are. In a different country or among different cultures, the best manners are those that are thoughtful, patient, and observant. What you don't know CAN hurt you.

On the *Tonight Show*

So maybe you aren't going to be on Rosie or Jay's show right away. You could land on television, though, as part of an event in your town or to be recognized for something you did after mastering $ecret Fourteen: Do Something. And whether there are 30 million people watching you or just 30,000, that's a lot of people to look ridiculous in front of. The indie woman who minds her manners need never look silly.

SCENARIO ONE

JAY: Please welcome, from Omaha, Nebraska, the town's leading Lionel train collector. Ms. Adams, I understand you have a train collection that winds through your house for a total of two miles. That's quite an achievement. Let's take a look at a clip of that collection. (Attention turns to the monitor.)

JAY: Ms. Adams, that's quite an effort. How much has this cost you?

MS. ADAMS: Actually, none of your business. Ask me something else.

JAY: Secretive, hmmm? Well, did you get any help building this?

MS. ADAMS: No, I did it all myself. That's a pretty condescending question, by the way.

JAY: Well Ms. Adams, why don't you tell us what inspired you to create such an ambitious model? (Meanwhile, he's signaling the crew to bring the next guest on early and get her OUT of there.)

SCENARIO TWO

JAY: Please welcome, from Omaha, Nebraska, the town's leading Lionel train collector. Ms. Adams, I understand you have a train collection that winds through your house for a total of two miles. That's quite an achievement. Let's take a look at a clip of that collection. (Attention turns to the monitor.)

JAY: Ms. Adams, that's quite an effort. How much has this cost you?

MS. ADAMS: Oh at least part of my paycheck for the last five years—I've put my heart and soul into this, as well as my savings.

JAY: It shows. Did you get any help building this?

MS. ADAMS: No, I did it all myself. Of course, you always have great ideas from everyone coming in, and I listen to them all—my whole family has been completely supportive.

JAY: Well Ms. Adams, why don't you tell us what inspired you to create such an ambitious model? (Meanwhile, he's signaling the crew to cancel the next guest and extend this segment.)

While you may not get a chance to be rude on Jay Leno, it's important to know how to field questions with grace. How you answer a question will determine if the interviewer will extend the interview or get rid of you as soon as possible. If you are making the interviewer look bad in front of his or her regular viewers, you will get neither thanks nor an invitation back!

Gear, Resources, and Actions for Minding Your Manners

Check Out These Books

DuPont, M. Kay. *Business Etiquette and Professionalism*. Menlo Park: Crisp Publications, 1998.

Martin, Judith. *Miss Manners' Basic Training: The Right Thing to Say*. New York: Crown, 1998.

Mitchell, Mary, and John Corr. *The Complete Idiot's Guide to Etiquette*. New York, Alpha Books, 1996.

Williams, Terrie. *Please and Thank You and Other Life Lessons for Teens*. New York: Scholastic, 2000.

Visit These Web Sites

Delphi Forum, **www.delphi.com/teen**

Kensington Etiquette, **www.kensingtonetiquette.com**

Call This Organization
Syndi Seid's Advanced Etiquette

(800) 276-7419

Try This

1. Practice the valuable art of introduction. Remember to take the time to properly introduce two people who don't know each other, by mentioning a topic of interest they may have in common.
2. Be polite! Listen to what people are saying to you; they won't fail to notice this genuine token of respect and you will be surprised at what you may learn from them.
3. Do you recall what your mother told you about slouching? She wasn't kidding, everyone reads body language. For one week, record instances in which your body language affected the outcome of your encounter. See if sitting up straight and looking interested really did make a difference in math class.
4. Record a conversation with:

    An elder
    A peer
    A parent

    In your exchanges were you rude? Polite? Whiny? Sincere? Generous? Could you have said that more respectfully?

Big $ecret Five:
Take Care of Yourself

In a way, all of the previous secrets are forms of taking care of yourself. But this BIG $ecret is an explicit demand to be mindful about yourself in a way that is not self-absorbed, but self-conscious; not egocentric, but wise. Taking care of others is one way we each reveal our humanity, it's another way of demonstrating that the universe is not just about ME. But taking care of ourselves is how we take responsibility for ourselves and show we are worthy of a spot on the planet. *Think of this secret as a positive form of selfishness.* If you are mindful of your needs, your health, and your point of view, you will be full of truth much of the time. And pursuing your truth is a very high form of independence.

Think about it. In all of the old fairy tales, the girl always waits to be rescued by someone else: Cinderella had to wait for a prince with a shoe; Snow White was first rescued by seven dopey dwarves, and then she was rescued again by another prince; Rapunzel had to wait until a prince climbed up her hair.

Getting rescued is expensive. It may look attractive at first glance, but think of the cost. Those fairy tales rarely tell you what happens after "happily ever after." I bet you don't remember that after Cinderella tried on the slipper and the prince saw that it fit, he went on a long journey, slaying dragons. She, however, was left to take care of his castle. (They didn't even have vacuum cleaners in those days.) He had adventure, and she had the cleaning chores. Snow White also ended up cleaning house. She had to work day and night to pay off those dwarves (don't tell me she really whistled while washing their old rags) and later, after the prince whisked her away, she discovered that he talked incessantly, was supermacho, and did not appreciate any of her talents. That was a bore. And after Rapunzel was rescued, she decided she wanted to cut her hair and her old prince had a fit.

Independence—the ability to rescue yourself—sometimes looks hard, but it's rarely as hard as living with the consequences of allowing others to determine what is right and true for you. Taking care of yourself, really, is a form of supernurturing. Who knows better than you how to take care of yourself? The next four secrets are all elements of taking good care of yourself.

17 $ecret

Get Tough

" I don't whine, I don't complain, I don't whimper. I work out. "
—Nadine Aurhammer

Look, you don't have to go to Marine boot camp or take up boxing (though one of my favorite DollarDivas did win the Golden Gloves Award in Chicago a few years ago). What I mean to say is that to have a free head and the independent spirit to follow your true path—regardless of the whims or approval of those around you—requires a serious amount of toughness: *stamina,* strength, and mental and emotional well-being.

If you play sports, you know what I'm talking about. If you're a writer, you know what I'm talking about. The kind of toughness divas nurture is the combination of a body that is in condition, a head that is well exercised (remember $ecret Five?), and a tuned-in awareness of one's own feelings. Strength doesn't come just from lifting free weights or being the leader everyone fears.

Your inner tranquillity, sense of humor, out-of-the-box way of looking at life, and your ability to handle stress are all elements of toughness that support the capacity for independence. When I asked a group of indie sisters what 10 things every independent femme should do, they all listed, "Learn to change a tire." Another popular item was, "Take the lid off the toilet tank and figure out how the flush works."

What they were all saying is that being helpless isn't part of the indie grrl's makeup. It's quite fine if someone is around and offers to help out in emergency situations. But standing by helplessly and hoping someone will rescue you is definitely not part of the indie package. So what is the formula for getting tough? Take it apart.

Physical Strength

I'm not talking about developing tight buns, or working off pounds, or trying to be some perfect (if illusory) weight. I'm talking about the muscle tone and endurance it takes to push yourself a little farther and a little harder than the next person, having that additional energy that will give you the edge for independence that the person beside you can't muster.

And I'm not interested in sounding like the surgeon general but you have to move to groove and what you eat will effect your feats. So here are 10 elements that are all part of getting tough, indie fashion.

1. Get Off the Couch
If you've been taking Ritalin since you were a kid, or you're one of those people who just can't sit still, skip this section. But if

curling up on the couch to watch the soaps or even to read for a few days is your idea of heaven, read on.

I'm a curler. Give me a warm patch of sun or a dark, cold day, and I don't want to do anything but bask in the sunlight or huddle under a warm blanket. So some days I do just that. (Why deprive myself of such basic pleasures? I'm a diva, I get to choose.)

But I do get off the couch a lot. On those sunny days I hike and use a rock I find on a canyon trail as my basking spot. On the cold days, I still hike—it warms me up, makes me feel as though I am transcending forces of nature. A gray, gloomy day becomes a textured, moody day—great weather for seeing the world in a different light, or capturing a great photographic moment.

It doesn't matter whether you play soccer or hike, bike or are an extreme snowboarder, the goal is to get off the couch, use your body, and make it know *you know* it's as sensitive as the engine of a 1962 Jaguar XKE.

An unused body disintegrates, and grows weak and wimpy. Whether you are in a wheelchair or are the fastest sprinter in the class, feel like a klutz or prefer to watch ice shows on TV rather than hit the ice yourself, you have to get off the couch and find some way to move your body.

2. Stretch

In the book, *Having Our Say: The Delaney Sisters First Hundred Years,* the true tale of two African-American sisters viewing their lives at 100-plus years of age, the 102-year-old points to her 104-year-old sister and explains, "Look, she started doing yoga religiously when she hit 50—that's why she looks so good."

Starting yoga in your early twenties won't make you live to 150, but it can't hurt. Stretching keeps you catlike and flexible. Touch your toes. Work on a back bend. The limber body is a strong body. The Origins stores sell a great little card you can stick in your purse or backpack, illustrating the major yoga movements. I take this card with me everywhere. And I never have the excuse of being without a yoga class or video—I have myself to rely on!

Any emergency you will ever have to meet (and there is an abundance of them in the course of a lifetime) is best met when your body responds with your head. Are you going to be the weak sister in the group when alarms start to ring, or are you going to be the leader who responds quickly and confidently to whatever situation arises?

3. Lift Weights

No, you won't develop triceps that make you look like Mr. World. You will shed fat and strengthen bones. You will increase your endurance and add a couple of hours to the energy you have to spend every day. And you will give yourself an edge with your newfound strength.

4. Breathe Hard

Aerobically, that is. The key is to increase your heart rate and exercise that most critical muscle. If you aren't about to sign up for Tae Bo or don't think you can get to the Y three times a week for a workout, then run, or find a set of stairs on which you can walk up and down for 20 minutes. Chase your dog around the park for a half hour. Skip rope.

5. Do Something Physical You Love

Find something that will last a lifetime. For some people it's tennis or golf. For others it's swimming or skiing. If you can't see yourself doing any of those things more than a couple of times a year, experiment until something does work for you.

Consider rock climbing, yoga, modern dance, archery, fencing, kayaking, or canoeing; windsurfing or sailing; hiking or badminton; volleyball or baseball; soccer or softball; rowing or wrestling. Identify anything physical you can imagine doing at least a couple of times a month with pleasure and anticipation and you have an instant catalyst to get you "off the couch." I'm a hiker. There are more trails and canyons near my home than I can explore in a lifetime. But Central Park and downtown Sydney offer equally challenging hikes—the secret is to view every trip as an expedition, missing nothing, soaking up details.

6. Keep a Food Journal

Our denial about what we eat is inspired. It's wonderfully easy to remember just the healthy things we eat and forget those frosted, sticky buns that were on the table this morning—too good to pass up.

I'm a little nervous about placing this element on the list. Too many women obsess about food, and food disorders are so common. But there is a profound difference between obsessing over calories and weight and being conscious of what you eat to keep your body healthy and strong.

Three thousand calories and a mountain of carbo-loaded pasta is not what keeps a body healthy for the long haul. Attention to finding delicious foods that are also great for the body is worth a little effort. But no one will ever become strong simply by following some extreme, deprivation-inspired diet. *Au contraire.*

Really healthy people are food connoisseurs. They love to cook often and find creative ways to prepare food that makes both the palate and the heart happy. Food is not something to avoid, but to understand, discover, and use like a palette of paints.

And when you keep a food journal—a daily diary of every morsel you place inside your own personal temple of a body— you receive a vivid look at what you are painting internally and a guide to what you may want to change or alter slightly. Think of the great female artist Mary Cassatt as your guide instead of Susan Powter—diet artists will chastise you to CONTROL yourself. But true artists encourage you to explore yourself. Find what works that is healthy. A food journal is a tool of exploration. Use it to make yourself strong.

7. Be Loyal to Your Body

Look, you've only got this one. It's possible you will be the first Bionic Woman off the set of a television series. You may see completely replicable body parts in your lifetime (Dolly the Sheep has made a giant contribution in this direction), but for the moment, we all need to honor and appreciate what we have.

To be independent you need a body you can count on. Whatever the capacity of your own body, you need to be true and loyal to it. Whether you are confined to a bed or a wheelchair, have incapacitating injuries or afflictions, or are in Olympic caliber physical shape, you have to be mindful of your one and only physical package. This is it. Take an oath. Sign up to take care of it every day.

8. Sleep

But you get by on four or five hours of sleep, have boundless energy, and even are able to pull the occasional all-nighter when you need to finish a project. You just don't NEED as much sleep as other people, you say. Maybe so, but that one and only body you have works overtime to pay for your careless disregard for its needs. Your cat can probably survive on a few meals a week, too, but do you really think you'd have a truly healthy cat in a year or two?

9. Avoid Body Toxins

This has nothing to do with your morality. A simple equation between strength and health requires that you limit body toxins to a minimum. (Besides, there is a total contradiction between being dependent on some toxins and being an indie girl, free of dependencies.)

Body toxins include: too much sugar, cigarettes (or anything else you inhale that doesn't have direct medical benefit), alcohol or drugs that aren't prescribed for specific needs, pesticides on food you don't bother to wash (those strawberries look divine, but did you run them through some water?), and excess of anything. (A box of chocolates or three meals in a row from your favorite fast food restaurant qualify as toxic excess!) When you're filling out your food journal, be sure you list all the toxins you ingest during a day—and over time, reduce them.

10. Get a Buddy

It's hard to be a lone soldier in the war for your body. Too much is poised against you: the fast food strip on the way home from work beckons when you are hungry and vulnerable. The late night ads for ice cream and gooey cheesy treats are aimed at sending you straight to the most decadent parts of the refrigerator.

Magazine ads and giant billboards are sirens of cool, enticing you to abandon your loyalty to your own body, while inviting you to be loyal to their products and their bottom line.

Even the weather can taunt you: it's too cold or too hot. It's raining or too windy to be out. And friends can be a real problem: "Come on, just a little longer," they plead, until getting to bed by 11:00 P.M. is a fantasy, and if you're lucky you shut off the light at 2:00 A.M. Or maybe everyone else is sitting around with a bottle of beer in their hands, and it feels strange to be the only holdout.

You need a buddy—or even better, several buddies. A peer group of divas is the best. But lacking that, you need at least one other human with whom you have a psychic agreement to pursue strength.

You harangue and encourage each other, support one another's great goals. If one of you is about to wimp out on that weekly game of tennis, the other is morally bound to drag the shirker off the couch. If you need help overcoming the tempting aroma of buttered popcorn at the movies, the buddy moves in and orders the small unbuttered carton.

It is not some inherent weakness in your character that makes taking care of your body a challenge. The world is ordered to undermine your strength, not build it. And to resist, you need a buddy.

Emotional Strength

Emotional strength is the capacity to be brave and not foolhardy; loving but not chronically needy; giving but not a doormat; strong but not hard. Indie women use their emotional strength to carry them through the really awful times that every life endures. Taking care of yourself emotionally is at least in part an exercise in self-awareness—an ability to set boundaries and make sure that everyone else's needs do not ALWAYS come first.

Check the following:
    ___ I assume I have a right to time alone.
    ___ I own my feelings and don't apologize for them.
    ___ I say no to family and friends without feeling guilty.
    ___ In the face of disaster I am the one who can handle crisis, not the one who needs to be rescued.
    ___ I handle pressure and usually do not crack under stress.
    ___ When under attack—personal, professional, or social/political—I hold my ground, I don't fold to my detractors.

A yes response to at least half these situations is a pretty good indicator that you have a healthy amount of emotional strength. Of course I'm not talking about becoming the kind of person who is ALWAYS under control—that's not emotional strength—that's called denial! If you don't cry when you're sad, feel scared in the face of danger, or have self-doubt when the road is rocky, you aren't human! But the emotionally strong person holds her own in the face of challenging situations.

I left a great job in a large company some years ago. I hadn't planned to make a big career change—and the prospect of leaving my VERY safe job filled me with terror. While I was trying to decide if I would make the change, I left work every night, went home to my very pleasant condo, just outside Harvard Square in Cambridge, Massachusetts, and cried.

At the end of the week, I stopped crying, made my decision, and got on with things. Some years later I am often asked the question, "How do you get over being scared?" (In relationship to making any kind of big change.) Now I answer: You don't. You just get used to it and know you won't die!

I often make big decisions with big consequences—if I came to a standstill every time I grew scared I'd never accomplish anything—but having exercised and developed some level of emotional strength, I can now plow forward with some confidence. And I watch my indie friends and know they do the same. So what are the exercises for emotional strength? Try the following suggestions for building your own emotional durability.

1. Ditch the Drama

DollarDivas do not screech at every surprise, whine over a chipped nail, or make everyone suffer with their endless list of inconveniences. There's a vast territory between hiding your feelings too much and making yourself the center of the universe all the time. Divas project a certain air of self-composure because they know the difference between life's small traumas and its big ones. Giving too much attention to the small traumas consumes energy that will be needed for the big ones, and indie grrls store up their energy by managing their dramas!

2. Meditate

Whether through prayer, meditation on a rock, repetition of a mantra, or observation of breathing, divas find the meditative state helps them reclaim their center, transcend life's static, and gain perspective on whatever annoying small stuff gets in their way.

3. Use Life's Bad News

Life has a way of humbling us, tearing us apart, sending extreme challenges we sometimes think are too much to bear. Whether it's the death of your loyal companion and best dog friend, the loss of a parent or lover, a disabling injury, or the loss of an opportunity you had counted on—these BIG traumas can make life seem truly dark and bleak. But I have come to see that I actually feel much more safe and comfortable now with people who have weathered the hard stuff. Independent women are not soft—they don't crack at the first emergency or loss because they have the inner spirit and compassion that comes from knowing, dealing, and transcending loss and disappointment.

Indie women are not professional or lifelong victims. They cope with whatever life hands them and use their experiences, no matter how grim, as character-building material. Consider the people in your own life. Can you tell the difference between those who have always been lucky, untouched by sadness, and those who have endured pain and found a way to rise above it?

4. Share

Nothing compares to a best friend to share your hopes, dreams, and plans with. And there's nothing like a team to work with in concert to achieve a goal. Indie women are not lone wolves. They are generous with their feelings, their ideas, and their experiences. Independent women are self-possessed and ABLE to function well on their own. But they also understand the need, indeed the value, of communicating and participating with others. Whether it's feelings of celebration and achievement or feelings of bereavement and sorrow, indie women are not afraid of sharing.

5. Focus

I have friends who have their fingers (and parts of their brain) in a hundred places at once. In part it's a lack of confidence (If I don't know what I want to do or what I care about, I want to keep my options open by having my hand in everything); in part it's a lack of discipline (I'm not willing to pay attention to one thing long enough to assess what is truly worth my attention). But the ability to focus is a key element of the DollarDiva's persona. And it is a critical ingredient for all the other $ecrets discussed in this book.

6. Find Open Windows

Part of emotional strength is the ability to find a sliver of light in the darkest situations. When the walls are falling in or the ship is sinking and everyone else is bailing, only the truly strong ones will look for the bricks to rebuild with or the log to float on. Giving up at the first sign of trouble or difficulty is NOT the brand of the indie grrl. Think about what opportunities lie in the following scenarios:

⦿ Joanna has been counting on going to grad school to study speech pathology since she was 16. A combination of scholarship money and savings have finally made that possibility a reality. Two weeks before she enters classes, her mother has a stroke and as an only child in a working-class family, it falls to Joanna to go home and care for her mother. What's the opportunity in this picture?

⦿ Natalie has been building her business for three years. This year she projects that her income from sales will break even with expenses and next year she will actually begin making substantial profits. Unexpectedly, a competitor comes to town with much deeper pockets than Natalie and by offering MUCH lower prices, drives her out of business. What's the opportunity here?

If you can find no serious opportunities in either of these all-too-common life events, you need to return to $ecret Seven: Get Out of the Box. Disaster—no matter how temporarily disabling—almost always has a flip side of opportunity. DollarDivas just seem to see those opportunities before others do.

Toughness doesn't come from lifting free weights or being stubborn. You may not plan to climb Mount Everest or build the next E-Bay, but if you have physical stamina and emotional strength—you COULD do both.

Gear, Resources, and Actions for Getting Tough

Check Out These Books

Brumberg, Joan Jacobs. *The Body Project: An Intimate History of American Girls.* New York: Vintage Books, 1998.

Carlson, Richard. *Don't Sweat the Small Stuff . . . and It's All Small Stuff.* New York: Hyperion, 1997.

Cooke, Kaz. *Real Gorgeous: The Truth about Body and Beauty.* New York: W.W. Norton & Co., 1996.

Maas, James. *Power Sleep: The Revolutionary Program That Prepares Your Mind for Peak Performance.* New York: Harper Collins, 1999.

Schwager, Tina, and Elizabeth Verdick. *The Right Moves, A Girl's Guide to Getting Fit and Feeling Good.* Minneapolis: Free Spirit Publishing, 1998.

Try These Organizations

Amateur Athletic Union of the U.S. Inc.

(800) AAU-4USA

www.aausports.org

AIDS Ride

(800) 825-1000

Walk for the Cure

Walk for the Cure is not a national organization, but segregated into many local communities and cities who run these walk/ride/bike for the cure programs. To find a local organization, type in "walk for a cure" and your city into a search engine.

The President's Council on Physical Fitness and Sports

(202) 690-5179

Visit These Web Sites

American Bicycle Association, **www.ababmx.com**

United States Fencing Association, **www.usfencing.org**

USA Gymnastics, **www.usa-gymnastics.org**

American Running and Fitness Association,
www.arfa.com

US Skiing and Snowboard Association, **www.usskiteam.com**

USA CUP, **www.usacup.com**

USA Triathlon, **www.usatriathlon.com**

Go Girl Magazine, **www.gogirlmag.com**

Just Sports for Women, **www.justwomen.com/contents.html**

GirlZone, **www.girlzone.com**

Try This

1. Find two destinations a week that you can get to by yourself, using your own two feet, a bit of creativity, and endurance.

2. Do sets of sit ups and leg or arm curls to maximize the

time while on the phone, watching TV, or listening to the radio.

3. Get off your butt! Take a self-defense class. Most communities, church organizations, or schools offer them at little or no cost.

4. Take your pet for a walk. If you don't have one, borrow one. It's a good way for you both to get exercise, and doesn't take too much time.

5. Register for a community taught CPR certification course. It won't cost too much money or time, and will benefit you as well as the community.

6. Last but not least, suck it up and donate a pint of blood twice a year.

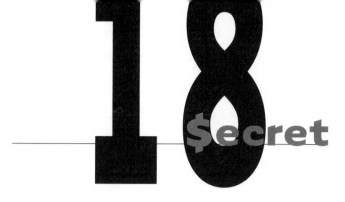

18 Secret

Cherish Friendships

"It's nice to make a friend, but it's awesome to have a friendship.
—SiBelle Israel

Nothing is as pathetic as a life without friendship—deep friendship, the kindred-souls kind of friendship. Independent women make great friends because they know how to be supportive when a friend is in need and know how to ask for help when they themselves are in need. Friendships make us richer, deeper, more interesting. And truly epic friendships are not necessarily with people who are just like us, but can be with people very different from ourselves, people who help us uncover different facets of our being.

Susan B. Anthony and Elizabeth Cady Stanton, partners in the quest for women's right to vote from the middle of the 19th century to well into the 20th, were also great and powerful friends—

who often disagreed on how to attain the vote and how to live. Their lifestyles were different, as were their tactics in dealing with others. But they were both deeply independent women, whose shared quest for independence for ALL women created a bond that lasted a lifetime.

Your friendships may not be so historically significant (though they might be!), but to be independent, you will need to nurture and value your friendships so that you can discover parts of yourself that only a friend who loves you enough to argue with you and accept you in all your guises, can unveil.

Gatekeepers

Bibianna Aroyo was a 1996 winner of the National Business Plan Competition for Teen Women. On the morning she was to be presented with her award, she attended a power breakfast with a group of distinguished business leaders, the people giving her the award, and her sister awardees.

The breakfast was held at an elegant hotel in Los Angeles, California. The conversation was thick with excitement and ideas. The business leaders made plentiful suggestions to the new awardees about people they should meet and opportunities available to them. Finally, as though her head were spinning, Bibianna looked around the table and blurted out: "I want this, I want *all* of this! How do I get it?!?"

What Bibianna was asking was, "How do I stay inside this circle, where opportunity and possibility seem greater and more tangible than I could ever have imagined?" Of course, the magic was that she was already there—the trick for her was not *how* to get in. She had done that by virtue of winning the award. The better questions were, "How do I stay in for life? How do I stay in touch with similar people who can open doors for me and help me make my life bigger than I had dared imagine possible?" Or,

"How do I build relationships with gatekeepers who can affect my life?"

Bibianna's wisdom in asking the question was profound. In addition to friendships that emerge naturally with our peers are the friendships that evolve with the gatekeepers in our lives. A gatekeeper is anyone who can help you gain access to an experience, information, or opportunities that are not easily available otherwise. Gatekeepers also have the ability to keep you OUT of places you may want to enter. With a single telephone call or a lift of an eyebrow they can make life easier or harder for you.

Gatekeepers can be mean-spirited or deeply generous. They may have the power of access as a function of their job (like the Dean of Admissions to a top college), their place in the community (everyone respects their opinion so their word carries weight), their circle of friends (she's a close friend of the newspaper editor, she might be able to arrange an interview), or their expertise (if your friend's sister is an expert in biochem and she sees you as having "potential" for the field, her word will have weight as a reference for you).

Almost everyone is a gatekeeper for something. You may be a gatekeeper yourself. Have you ever opened a door for anyone? If your mother ever told you "not to burn your bridges" she meant in part that you never know how today's enemy can be helpful to you tomorrow!

Obviously you shouldn't spend your life building friendships with everyone based on what they might be able to do for you. But as you meet people throughout your life, there are two things to keep in mind that will help you build bridges you can cross as the need arises.

The first is curiosity. You can't know a person's power if you don't know anything about him or her. *The world is not always about you.* Make sure you spend time uncovering other people's stories to find out who they are and what is important to them. But remember, collecting stories only to figure out what someone might do for you is not the point. That sort of egocentricity will serve you poorly! If you are so caught up in your own story that you don't ask about others, you, as an aspiring actor, may never know that the person sitting beside you is on the board of a repertory theater and friends with the director of casting calls. Or if your heart is set on being the lead vet for the San Diego Zoo someday, it might be nice to know that the person you have been insulting all evening is the daughter of one of the leading contributors to the zoo!

Curiosity about other people will bring you rewards in ways you cannot imagine. It will also give you clues, small gems of information you can store away for a future time when you might open a door for someone else, or ask for one to be opened for you.

This leads to the second thing to remember in regard to gatekeepers: reciprocity—mutual dependence, action or influence shared, felt, or shown by both sides. That is, I never think of what others might do for me without giving equal thought to what I might do for them. Acts of reciprocity demonstrate that you are not simply an ambitious little beaver, ready to exploit anyone for your own advancement, but are thoughtful and appreciative of opportunities made available to you, truly, from the heart. Nothing will close gates faster than a cunning, self-serving quest for advantage by someone who has no one else's concerns in mind but her own.

How to Enhance Your Opportunities

So let's assume you have the heart to deserve the aid of gatekeepers, and the generosity of spirit to be a good one yourself. Now what? Bibianna, if you are reading, this list is for you. This is the list that answers your question: How do I get this? The guide below may seem foolishly simple—but these ingredients make the difference between people who seem to have "good luck," and those who have none at all. It's the difference between the self-confident, and the proud but isolated loner.

1. Build Your Rolodex

My friend Inabeth Miller has three giant Rolodex card files on her office desk. She has two more at home. And of course she has an entire database on her computer as well. Inabeth is a magical gate-keeper—and a gifted one—who seems to have a sixth sense about who needs to meet whom. If I get stuck on a problem, I can always call her and she will pull a name from her Rolodex, and suddenly I have information, or access to information, I need.

My Rolodex may never be as full as Inabeth's but it is different. I have different friends, contacts, and acquaintances, and she knows that I will be as generous with my contacts as she is with hers. Now, my own Rolodex is a resource for myself. Notes on the backs of the cards I have gathered give me information about the people I meet, where I met them, and what they are interested in. Sometimes when stuck on a problem, I thumb through my Rolodex and am reminded of people I already know who can help me with a problem or an opportunity.

2. Master the "Power Lunch"

Assuming you acquire the practiced grace of business etiquette (if there is any doubt, sign up for a course right away!), it's time to understand the power of breaking bread and its relevance to the independent woman. A "power lunch" (or breakfast or tea or dinner, for that matter) is a shared meal with a purpose. Food is central to building relationships. It is fraught with ritual and symbolism. We talk about "breaking bread" as a way to create a bond; we share meals and share a measure of intimacy. Food relaxes almost everyone (unless you're obsessing about how to became thinner and thinner and food makes you crazy—then you have to choose between thin and power; call me crazy but power is a little more attractive in my head).

So imagine this: You have an idea for a project that would turn a tennis tournament into a fundraiser to feed the homeless in your community. Or you have an idea for a new software application. How are you going to enlist support? How will you get advice and how are you going to convince your friend's mother, who happens to be close to the head of sales for a major software distributor, to introduce you to her contact at the company? Of course, a "power lunch." You must consider:

- those with whom you want to get together—the gate-keepers to your goals,
- what you want from the meeting (money, ideas, help, introductions?),
- where you want to meet,
- how to make the process work to achieve your goal, and
- how to follow up.

Let's start with *who:* first, don't allow anything to get in the way of your guest list. Consider your goals and who might help you reach them—or who might know someone who can help you reach them. I like to manage four to six people for a "power lunch"—but with time you'll figure out your own favorite number.

What do you want from the meeting? Make sure you know. You can't fritter away people's time. It is the stuff most jealously guarded, even more than money—so if someone joins you for lunch, or breakfast or tea, make sure you have a plan for how to use the time smartly. Waste it and you're toast. Make sure everyone knows what you expect from the meeting. Do you want to build relationships? Do you want feedback for an idea? Do you need someone to pitch in and do something? You may need all of the above, but be clear and be conscious that bringing people on board with an idea is a time-consuming process. You may need several meetings. Think it through.

Where are you going to meet? Maybe you can't afford to charge lunch to your credit card. Here are some options: find a friend or supporter who *does* have the ability to host several people for lunch and who supports your idea to host the lunch; see if a friend will act as "chef" and create a meal that can be held at your home; invite guests to a bag lunch at a quiet table in the park—bring a tablecloth, napkins, and flowers to turn it into your own "power spot." These ideas may not be conventional, but if your invitation is clear and your plan is a good one, you'll get a response. Never *assume* that someone else will pick up a check—if they don't and you have to ask them to, it wasn't really an invitation, was it?

Manage the process. Make sure everyone knows one another at the table.

- Give time for people to introduce themselves and talk about why they might be interested in the agenda for the meeting.

- Make sure everyone has airtime but remember it's your job to keep the conversation on track for your goal.

- Listen. Remember, you invited people for their help/ideas/thoughts—not so that you could consume all the airtime.

- Be sure to ask for what you need. If you don't ask, you won't get it; people do not read minds. And the people you most want at a power lunch are the busiest people—they won't offer help unless you ask for it!

- Make it fun! People won't return for a second meeting if you bore them at the first. (Would you?)

Follow up. Make sure you have their business cards and have given one of your own. (A calling card may be just the thing.) Send a note thanking them for their ideas, following up on any suggestions, or otherwise showing you were paying attention!

3. Be a Great Protégée

Most people (unless they are distinctly warped) enjoy watching others succeed. If they can be a part of that success, the satisfaction is amplified. Good mentors are not looking for someone who will need them constantly. (If they are, get away fast!) They are not looking for someone to grow into the image of themselves. Great mentors aren't looking for someone who will be *dependent* on them, but instead for someone who can grow and become more independent as they blossom.

You should be able to build relationships with one or more mentors who take pleasure in your development as a separate, distinct person with original ideas and the capacity for action. Make sure you thank your mentor for the gift of their wisdom and advice.

Gear, Resources, and Actions for Cherishing Friendships

Check Out These Books

Berry, Carmen Renee, and Tamara Traeder. *Girlfriends: Invisible Bonds, Enduring Ties.* Berkeley, CA: Wildcat Canyon Press, 1995.

Catalyst, Sheila Wellington. *Creating Women's Networks: A How-To Guide for Women and Companies.* San Francisco: Jossey-Bass Publishers, 1998.

Mason, Marilyn. *Seven Mountains: The Inner Climb to Commitment and Caring.* New York: Dutton Books, 1997.

Visit These Web Sites
www.bizwomen.com

www.girlsite.com

www.webgrrls.com

See These Videos
Now and Then, 1995.
Beaches, 1988.

Try This
Create a "map" of your friends, with you at the center of the map. Draw a circle and place your closest friends there. Keep adding circles, placing friends, gatekeepers, mentors, acquaintances. Are you neglecting anyone? Are you overlooking friends who may also be gatekeepers?

Revel in Solitude

"Thinking and relaxing on your own can help you deal with life. It's time to reflect and get away from the stress of daily life."
—Erin Connolly

I grew up spending summers on a crystalline lake in central Maine. There were few children my age, and I had endless hours to explore by myself the paths and inlets of that magic pond. Solitude for me will always conjure up the exotic smell of water lilies, the wail of the loon, still glass-like water broken occasionally by the rocks I skipped across its surface, and the smell of pine.

But long before I was there, Henry David Thoreau, in his book, *The Maine Woods,* described another girl who lived in this very place I grew up:

> Near where we landed [in the canoe] sat an Indian girl, ten or twelve years old, on a rock in the water, washing, and humming a song meanwhile.

No more was said about this girl. He went on to write about visiting with her father and others in the village. Thoreau wrote *The Maine Woods* in 1846. But most writers didn't think girls were worthy of comment then. That Thoreau noticed her at all speaks to the power of her image on that rock. When I think of that girl, I wonder if the solitude of the water and her rock were like mine. I wonder what she thought about and felt as she sat there alone on her rock, humming with the water.

Independent women are not always alone. Sometimes rarely alone. As I pointed out in the introduction, true independence is not about being alone, it is about being independent in the context of others: family, friends, community. One doesn't have to be a hermit to be independent.

But solitude and the enjoyment of it is critical to the blossoming of the independent spirit. Learning to entertain oneself and make use of hours alone is yet another secret of independent women. It is impossible to build a business, create an important work of art, invent a new vaccine, write a poem, or develop oneself in any way at all, without the experience of being with oneself.

There is a difference between solitude and simply being alone. If you find yourself alone and bored on a Saturday afternoon and are restless and cranky because plans fell through or you didn't think to make them in advance, you are not gaining the joys of solitude, you are fretting about being alone. There is major difference between these two states.

In the "fretting because I'm alone" state, the mind is full of static, like a TV station that goes off in the night while the TV is still on, crackling with energy but not making anything useful of the energy. In solitude, the energy is quiet, strong, focused. Independent people use solitude as an energy source the way our body uses sugar for energy. Without time to tap into the energy of solitude, independent people risk losing their sense of direction, clarity, and access to their inner voice.

I make my biggest mistakes when either I cannot hear my inner voice or worse, hear it and ignore it. I have finally learned (though I sometimes still forget temporarily) that if I don't immediately know what to do about something I should wait until I can find some modicum of solitude in which I can be still and listen to what my inner voice is saying. Most successful women will say the same. But that has taken years to learn. How can you do it earlier? How can you use solitude to develop your independence?

Watch a cat. My cat is a great tutor in the art of solitude. Too much frenetic energy in the house? People visiting she doesn't feel a good vibe from? She retreats to a small nook of quiet solitude. (There's a spot under my bed she likes a lot.) She isn't frightened, she just chooses not to engage right then. She is highly judicious about how and with whom she will share her precious time and energy.

When I meditate, she meditates. She's more disciplined than I am. I can be distracted by sounds outside the window or thoughts that pull me out of the meditation. She gives herself over to the meditative state with complete commitment. And when I stretch to return to activity, she stretches longer and is more the yoga master than I will ever be.

She's young still, so she's playful, sometimes utterly wild, racing around the house doing outrageous things to attract my attention. But when she's ready to spend some time with herself, she relaxes into her solitude. Her muscles are at rest, she breathes easily. My attempts to distract her are futile. A daily dose of solitude is a pleasure for this cat.

But what if you HATE being alone? The sound of silence makes you anxious. What if an hour of solitude makes all your mental monsters appear?

Test your own tolerance for solitude with these questions:

1. **yes** ___ **no** ___ Do I spend at least an hour contentedly alone in a week?

2. **yes** ___ **no** ___ When I'm alone do I need to call someone right away?

3. **yes** ___ **no** ___ When I'm alone do I need to get busy immediately?

4. **yes** ___ **no** ___ When I'm alone do I entertain myself easily?

5. **yes** ___ **no** ___ When I'm alone do I feel at peace?

6. **yes** ___ **no** ___ Do I ever eat alone in restaurants, happily?

7. **yes** ___ **no** ___ Do I go to the movies by myself—and enjoy it?

8. **yes** ___ **no** ___ Have I recently taken a long walk by myself?

If you marked "no" three or more times, you have some work to do on developing your tolerance and your use of the power of solitude.

Up to this point, the secrets I've revealed have all been action-oriented. Developing economic power, being willing to break rules, reading, exploring, building critical relationships—these are all action heroine roles. The yang of independence.

Solitude is the yin, the other side. One must be able to do things, to act, to become independent. But the power to be still and quiet is likewise necessary. Solitude is not a punishment. It is a gift, a source of magic. You can and *must* tap it—you won't be really independent until you do.

Eight Steps to Loving Solitude

If being alone makes you antsy and nervous, take these steps toward improving your peace of mind and being at ease with yourself—and by yourself:

1. Practice short intervals of solitude—say 10 to 15 minutes a day at first.

2. Find a place where you love to practice—for me it was the lily pond near my family's camp. For you it might be your bedroom, a particular chair in the house, a park bench under a protective old tree, a special rock on a path you frequent. It should be accessible, beautiful, and memorable. Now when I am in the middle of my wildest days, I can still find solitude in my mind's eye, just by remembering the details of that exquisite lily pond.

3. Settle in to your place and take a long, deep breath. Do that a few times.

4. Now listen. Just listen. Forget yourself and just listen to what is (or is not) around you.

5. Look. Take in the colors, the details of the place where you are. Be slow in your observations. Build awareness of your surroundings as if you were Sherlock Holmes's sister. Solitude can help you get outside yourself, not just focus egocentrically on yourself.

6. Okay, so now you know where you are. You are grounded. Take your eyes off your watch and just sit quietly for a bit. If something comes to mind that makes you anxious, release it. Take deep breaths again, listen, and look around. Let your mind wander. See what comes up, don't fret over it, just let thoughts come and go, like ripples in a pond.

7. When a little time has passed and you're ready to reenter the busy world, take a deep breath and stretch—like a cat.

8. And one more thing—if you have friends who cannot stand being alone for any amount of time, be wary—they may swallow up your time, just so they do not

have to deal with their own disquiet. If someone, male or female, wants to absorb every minute of your time, set some boundaries—these people will undermine your best attempts at making time to be with yourself.

Solitude can take many forms and offer a variety of benefits over time. For some, solitude is experienced in the presence of beauty; for others, time with nature is important; and for still others, meditation and prayer are crucial.

Some of my best ideas come to me when I am hiking alone or sitting quietly watching waves. And listen to how Alix Kates Schulman (the author of *Memoirs of an Ex-Prom Queen*) describes her experience of solitude. After leaving New York City, and a life filled with action, noise, celebrity, and stimulation, for an isolated island on the Maine coast, she finds:

> Solitude its own reward! Instead of making me anxious, it seems to be sweeping away my anxieties, opening up possibilities . . .[1]

If I have been cranky and snarling at people all day, I use solitude to help me focus on the real source of my disquiet. Usually the people I'm behaving badly with are not the real problem!

And sometimes solitude simply helps me replenish my energy. If it has been a mad week of meetings, gatherings of people, endless phone conversations, too many commitments and places to be, there comes a point when all the stimulation, no matter how exciting or wonderful it may be, is just too much. I remember my cat and find a quiet place to retreat, to gather myself to myself again. You, too, can be a like a cat and carry the inner grace of solitude with you at all times.

"Being alone is a gift I give myself. By taking time to be with my thoughts and dreams while engaging in some activity that requires no words (gardening, hiking, painting), I renew myself and replenish that which I have to offer to all my relationships."
—Annie Fox, Electric Eggplant Entertainment

---

1. Schulman, Alix Kates. *Drinking the Rain*. NY: Penguin, 1996.

Gear, Resources, and Actions for Reveling in Solitude

Check Out These Books

Breathnach, Sarah Ban. *Simple Abundance: A Daybook of Comfort and Joy.* New York: Warner Books, 1995.

McCairen, Patricia. *Canyon Solitude: A Woman's Solo River Journey Through the Grand Canyon.* Seattle, WA: Seal Pr. Feminist Publishing, 1998.

Shulman, Alix Kates. *Drinking the Rain.* First ed. New York: Farrar, Straus and Giroux, 1995.

Slocum, Capt. Joshua. *Sailing Alone Around the World.* First American ed. New York: London, Norton, 1984. New York: Dover Publications, 1998.

Taylor, Jill McLean, Carol Gilligan, Amy M. Sullivan. *Between Voice and Silence: Women and Girls.* Cambridge, Mass: Harvard University Press, 1995.

Thoele, Sue Pattonn, Jennifer Louden. *The Women's Book of Soul: Meditations for Courage, Confidence & Spirit.* Berkeley, CA: Conari Press, 1998.

Visit These Web Sites

Starlight Café, **www.starlitecafe.pair.com/tales2/ Friends.html**

Travelin' Ladies, **www.committment.com/travel.html**

Listen to This Music

The Book of Secrets, Loreena McKennitt

Solitude Standing, Suzanne Vega

Shepherd Moons, Enya

20 $ecret

Let Go

" Give expecting nothing in return."
—Valjeanne Estes

The last secret to be divulged is possibly the most important—and the most curious. The previous secrets are connected in one way or another to action, leadership, being in control. The conundrum of independent women is that they achieve those qualities—but also manage somehow to let go, to be less concerned about where they are going and more concerned about the nature of their journey. Is it possible to do both? DollarDivas prove it is. By not clinging to things that sap energy uselessly, they take care of themselves—making room for love, health, caring, and for making a difference.

What exactly do you need to let go of? Six big items appear on the list of things you can give up, making room for your independence to soar:

1. Perfection
2. Anger
3. Certainty
4. Harmful habits
5. Self pity
6. Things

In the interest of candor, let me acknowledge that, independent woman though I am, I am not a perfect role model; I have not let go of all these things—or maybe it's better to say that some days I am able to let go of things more easily than I can on other days. This is a journey—not a destination; a life's work—not a weekend assignment. So as you make your own efforts, be forgiving of yourself . . . and know that independent women are flawed and human—not paragons of . . .

Perfection

Each of the other nineteen $ecrets urges you to attain skills, knowledge, attitude, or experience. In doing that, the implication is that you can *completely* accept your weirdness or that you can be an expert investor or an extremely aware political activist. Of course the aim is important—if you are studying to be a veterinarian or a house painter I want to know you will be as expert as possible. If you are using your voice to be heard on an issue of importance, I hope you will be strong, loud, and compelling. Whatever you do should be done with excellence as the goal.

But a lot of B and C students are running large companies, color-blind women with no fashion sense have great panache and the ideal of perfection is just that, an ideal—a place you are trying get to but may never reach . . . and that's the joy!

It's one thing to fuss over not having tried hard to win a race, get the highest grade point average in your school, or meet that deadline at work, but it is folly to dwell over not *being* perfect—a waste of energy, a self-indulgent activity that gets you no closer to the goal and consumes energy better used elsewhere.

Independent women are not slaves to perfection. To give up perfection is not to abandon your dreams, but to tune in to what is possible to do today and to be loving and accepting of the gifts you are able to contribute.

I said at the beginning of this chapter that I am not a perfect role model—but, I have not given up my desire to BE a perfect role model. On my saner days I remember that role models must model humanity—and I do that extremely well!

The table that follows is a truthful assessment of where I think I am on my goals relative to the quest for perfection. Use the blank table beneath it to create your own.

My Map

Goals	Level of Perfection (1–10)	Things I do to keep me on my journey
Being a good leader for my company	8	I watch other good leaders. I read about great leaders. I check in with the people I lead. I attend retreats and conferences for leaders.
Managing my diet and exercise	7	I visit my doctor regularly—he acts like part of my conscience! I keep a food/exercise journal (so I don't try to kid myself). I hang out with people who care about fitness.

| Keeping a clean house | 7 | I just remember that I can't write when my living space is chaos—so if I want to get anything on paper, I have to have an orderly environment! |
| Staying in touch with my friends | 6 | The death of my best friend a few years ago was a shocking and dreadful reminder of how brief life can be. We shouln't all need such a reminder to stay in touch with cherished friends. . . . |

Your Map

Goals	Level of Perfection (1–10)	Things I do to keep me on my journey

Am I going to get upset because I have no 10s on this table? Of course not. The 6 is there because of the 8 at the top. Maybe next year I'll have a 9 in the first box. By being a more efficient leader I can also be a better friend, increasing that number to 8 or 9. But the truth is I need all of my energy to deal with what is already on my plate. Squandering energy by focusing on how badly I've managed doesn't help me improve, it only depletes energy that is needed in other places. In this way, I have given up perfection, even if I never give up the quest for it.

Anger

There are days when I get *sooo* angry. I stew and sputter and talk about why I am so mad. I explain to anyone who will listen all the reasons for my perfectly legitimate anger. I replay the source of my anger over and over in my mind's eye. I think of all the smart things I COULD have said, COULD have done to get revenge or pursue justice. Coulda, woulda, shoulda.

These are, of course, my least productive days. All Zen-warrior independent women know this. It always helps to see someone else who is angry.

Mad Martha has just heard that a colleague received a fellowship that she had been counting on. Furious, she calls five friends and complains: "I don't know what they were thinking. Jackie has none of the experience I have. She must have an in with the selection committee. I'm going to make sure that she is not invited to the meeting next week to select a new director for the center. In fact, I'm going to make sure she isn't invited to anything having anything to DO with the center! Can you imagine WHY they selected her??"

By using her energy to punish Jackie for getting an opportunity she wanted, Mad Martha starts to look like a bad-spirited nut. And, she uses valuable time she instead could use to apply for another fellowship, or find out what she needs to do to be selected for the fellowship next time. Living life as an angry person is exhausting. And after a while, people avoid you—they don't want to be around "bad energy."

This doesn't mean that you can't get angry. Some of my BEST ideas have been formed during a moment of anger. Instead of wasting time seeking revenge or retribution, I channel all that delicious energy into creativity! In fact, I have come to see my creative energy as whining turned inside out. Whiners are *sooo* unattractive and boring to be around. They complain until you are sick of hearing them, but rarely have any ideas about what to do to change whatever they are whining about.

How can you convert these sources for legitimate anger into creative energy?

- That guy you've been seeing lately doesn't call for a week, and you find out he was dating a friend of yours.
- Your history professor makes a snide remark about you in class, and you feel completely foolish.
- Your mother is an alcoholic, and she embarrasses you in front of your friends.
- The school principal makes a crack that was extremely racist.
- A good friend takes an idea you had been working on and appropriates it for herself, receiving all the glory for it as well.

The important thing to remember about anger is that you have choices:

1. You can get caught up in it, allowing it to eat at you and take a double toll. (The original offense and then all your energy spent to deal with the issue.)
2. You can get over it—moving on to more important ways to spend your energy.

3. Or, you can use the angry energy to create something
    original, positive, and useful.

Independence is a function of not being held captive by things
you cannot control. I'm always amazed (and impatient) whenever
I am in public and have the unhappy occasion to observe an angry
person rattling on about something minor that ticked them off.
"GET OVER IT," I want to scream, "WHO CARES?!" Letting
go of anger is the only way you can acquire energy to pursue the
other $ecrets.

Certainty

There is none. Physicists and astronomers admit that they know
less about the universe today than they ever did. The more they
learn, the less they know. (This makes them very happy, by the
way—it means it's an exciting era for scientists—maybe E.T. is out
there somewhere!)

Computer geniuses have no clue about the long-term impact
of the Internet. My grandfather often predicts the weather as well
as most meteorologists—and that's about 75 percent of the time.
Do you know what your best friend will be doing in 10 years?
Are you sure you will be living in the same town five years from
now?

We all search for answers. (It's scary to think no one is smart
enough to have all the answers!) This explains why faith is powerful, why the Church of Scientology has so many followers, why
books that sell *Six Ways to Get Rich* are such a hit. In an uncertain
and risky universe we all want to cling to something.

I use my routines like lighthouses along a strange shore. If I've
been traveling for a few weeks and am deprived of my orderly
routine of morning coffee, newspaper, shower, and Protein Fruit
smoothie—all in a certain order—I became cranky. I want some-

thing in my life to be sure and steady, and when even my silly routines fail me, I feel off-balance. A degree of certainty can be extraordinarily comforting. But even when I think I have something certain to hang on to for a while, I try to remind myself not to get too attached.

I learned my best lesson about certainty as a young woman working at the Polaroid Corporation. I was asked to be a part of a project team working on a new product. It was an exciting and prestigious assignment, and I leaped at the opportunity. But when the project was finished, I had no official or permanent job—*no certainty* about what I would do next, or even if there WOULD be a job for me.

The person to whom I reported met with me and gave me three choices:

1. Return to the job I had been doing before the special assignment (a job that now seemed incredibly humdrum and boring).
2. Take a different job working for him (a job that would also be safe, but probably fairly dull as well).
3. Or, "wait and see what comes up."

Yuck, I remember the way my stomach felt when I understood that my choices were either one of two possibly boring jobs or a period of ambiguity in which nothing might happen and I would have NO job, unless I was lucky and something interesting came up. Though I could see this manager thought ambiguity was as much fun as a bike trip in the south of France, it didn't really feel good to me—I wanted certainty. But, of course, I was a little spoiled and also wanted a great next assignment. I took his third option.

I can't say I enjoyed hanging out on a tightrope without a net, but I did get an idea for a great next project and, armed with research and a proposal, received permission to make that my next job. That assignment eventually led to the creation of my first company—something I had never envisioned for myself.

At most "DollarDiva" conferences, we run Rotating Interview Sessions. Participants have an opportunity to interview three to four successful business women and role models in the course of an hour. At the end of that time they are asked: What surprised you most about the women you met? Almost universally, we hear: none of them are doing what they thought they would be doing when they were younger! Certainty—even about our career—is a fluid and changing thing. Life would be boring if we DID know everything for certain—the adventure is in the surprises!

Certainty is an illusion. Even people who think they will find a nice safe job in the post office, or as a tenured professor, or working in a big company, close their eyes to the reality that life happens. Post offices consolidate. Schools close or eliminate entire departments. Companies merge. The best offense for certainty is independence—relying on yourself to create answers from within rather than spending energy seeking them all around you.

Harmful Habits

We all have our vices. Some people smoke, other people drink too much, some overindulge in sugar, while others defy the odds in extreme ways that seem to tempt the fates. Extreme overeating and extreme undereating are sports that have serious drawbacks.

Pick your poison. Harmful habits are as varied as the people who indulge in them. What's yours, and what function does it serve? If it's completely harmless and works for you in some way, it's probably not an issue. Your mother may nag you to stop "twirling" your hair, but if you're not pulling it out, what's the harm?

Most habits have some consequence. If it's not serious, it probably isn't worth getting too concerned. But you need some sense of the costs and the drawbacks of your habits to help you decide whether you need to spend energy undoing them. Here's a chart you can use to get a grip on your vices.

Vice	Benefits	Drawbacks	Impact	Plan
Drinking				
Smoking				
Overspending				
Interrupting others				
Eating too much/too little				

Now obviously, no neat chart is going to make giving up deeply desired and ingrained habits an easy task. They're habits precisely because you don't want to give them up! But if you bring them to the front of your attention, you can take action.

That's the secret of the independent woman—not that she doesn't have harmful vices, but that she has made herself aware of them, understands the impact they have on her (and on the people who care about her), and has a plan to address them. Whether it's the help of a buddy or a specialist, work with someone who can help you make a difference. The independent woman is the one in charge of her harmful habits.

Self-pity

Poor me . . . life is soooo hard. I have such bad luck. I've experienced so many losses. Things never seem to turn out well for me . . .

There is a terrific children's book called *Alexander and the Terrible, Horrible, No Good, Very Bad Day* by Judith Viorst. In it, Alexander, the little boy of the title, has a tough day. Whatever can go wrong does. At the end of every unfortunate episode he says: "It's been a terrible, horrible, no good, very bad day. I'm going to Australia." In Alexander's mind there must be somewhere else to go where things could be better, "if only—"

A few years ago I was vacationing in the British Virgin Islands. I spent an afternoon at one of those perfect beach bars—where the wind is gentle, the reggae rocked, and people were coming and going from their boats and the beach. As the afternoon wore on (I was pretty lazy that afternoon), I had a chance to talk with the owner. It turned out he had grown up on the island and all of his family were still there. But he had lived in many parts of the world, worked at a variety of jobs, and had led a life full of opportunity and excitement.

"What brought you back to this small, sleepy island?" I asked.

His answer was wonderfully wise: "I traveled all over the world thinking the grass was always greener on the other side of the fence," he said. "Then I finally figured out that if I just watered my own yard, I'd have green grass, too."

And indeed he had. His beach restaurant/bar was one of the most popular on the island—not the biggest or the fanciest—but the friendliest, the most comfortable, the one you think of when you dream of a perfect slow afternoon with good music in the Virgin Islands!

Independent women know this, too. Whining is so boring. Poor me is such a drag. Self-pity is a waste of energy. Not happy with the way your lawn looks? Do something about it! The person who lets go of self-pity is the one who can achieve miracles with a dead lawn.

Life is not easy. Stuff happens. People die, great opportunities vanish, natural disasters occur, illnesses strike, friends betray. All these things can befall any one of us. Sometimes all in the same month. Indie women are more creative than other people when it comes to turning terrible into terrific. They have little time for self-pity, because they are so busy figuring out how to make their grass "greener."

Ten Ways to Make Your Lawn Greener

1. **Turn it into a Japanese Zen garden planted with jade.**
2. **Water it.**
3. **Fill it with ivy.**
4. **Wear green eyeshades.**
5. **Use fertilizer.**
6. **Turn it into a water garden, planted with big, green lily pads.**
7. **Create a frog farm. Put hundreds of sculpted frogs on your lawn.**
8. **Paint it.**
9. **Put down sports turf.**
10. **Treat it with loving care.**

Gear, Resources, and Actions for Letting Go

Check Out These Books

Basco, Monica Ramirez. *Never Good Enough: Freeing Yourself from the Chains of Perfectionism.* New York: Simon & Schuster, 1999.

O'Halloran, Susan, and Susan Delattre. *The Woman Who Found Her Voice: A Tale of Transforming.* Philadelphia, PA: Inisfree Publishing, 1997.

Smith, Betty. *A Tree Grows in Brooklyn.* New York: Harper Collins, 1998.

Visit These Web Sites

Teen Advice Online, **www.teenadvice.org**

Working with Groups to Overcome Panic, Anxiety, and Phobias, **www.wholeperson.com/wpa/ghb/gpp/toc.htm**

The Biggest
$ecret of ALL

> "You already are an inde-pendent woman."

You have all the potential, possibility, and capacity to be a unique, fully developed, one-of-a-kind indie woman. All the secrets in this book exist in some form within you. Your work is simply to uncover the seedlings of your own independent qualities and nourish them.

All the DollarDivas described and talked about in this book are "works in progress." As you are. There is no Perfect 10 for independence. Some days we're a 4 or a 6, others days a 12! Some days our best work is in being fully dependent and allowing others to take care of us. Who we are each day is an ever-changing reality. But independent women have aims; they hold a vision of themselves in their mind's eye that they can see almost all the time.

This book is meant to be used and reused over time. The independent qualities you have today will be deeper in a year, and deeper and more complex three years after that.

Your brand of independence may look different from your best friend's. It may be different still from that of your great charismatic aunt who seems so self-assured and independent. Remember $ecret One: Embrace Your Weirdness. The great fingerprint of your soul is your personal style—your own kind of independent spirit. And remember that others will look up to you, so make sure they see something high and grand!

About the Author

Joline Godfrey is the CEO and founder of Independent Means Inc., providing programs and products for the financial novice. She is also the author of *Our Wildest Dreams: Women Making Money, Having Fun & Doing Good,* as well as *No More Frogs to Kiss: 99 Ways to Give Economic Power to Girls.* She lives in Ojai, California, where she hikes, lives with a zencat, and practices the secrets she writes about. You can visit her at **www.dollardiva.com.**